A.S.P.I.R.E.

Because S.M.A.R.T. Goals

Are Dumb

Nicholas P. Hughes

Nicholas P Hughes, Kokoro Press

17115 Kenton Dr, Apt 302A

Cornelius, NC 28031

www.NickHughesCoaching.com

Book Layout ©2017 BookDesignTemplates.com

Ordering Information:

Quantity sales. Special discounts are available on quantity purchases by corporations, associations, and others. For details, contact the "Special Sales Department" at the address above.

ASPIRE/ Nicholas Hughes. —1st ed.

ISBN 978-0-9858565-2-6

Dedicated to everyone who got suckered into S.M.A.R.T. goals and to everyone who has set goals and then beaten themselves up when they didn't get done.

Where There Is No Vision,

The People Perish.

—PROVERBS 29:18

Contents

WHY MOST GOAL-SETTING SYSTEMS DON'T WORK

D oes this sound familiar? Like millions of other people around the world, on the first of January, you write out your annual goals.

You set bold intentions. This is the year you'll finally lose the weight, quit smoking, start the side hustle, ask for a raise, buy a new car, travel the world, and run a marathon. You're not just going to set these goals; you're going to crush them.

You throw out the junk food, buy new running gear, join the gym, toss the cigarettes, make the business plan, rehearse your *"I'd like a raise speech,"* haunt the car dealerships, surf the web for your dream destinations, and start mapping out your marathon training route.

For a week or two, you're killing it. You've lost two pounds, you've only had a few cigarettes, saved fifty bucks towards your dream vacation, made it to the gym, and waited to share the equipment with all the other hopefuls.

And then, the inevitable. The scales creep back up. You've skipped the gym, your running gear is still in the wash (besides, your calf muscles are really sore), and you're back to the grind.

You feel like Sisyphus. Endlessly pushing the boulder up the hill, only to watch it roll back down. How many years have you been doing this?

Stuff it. You can always start again next year, right?

The only good thing about this is you're not alone. Just about everyone else in the world has done precisely the same thing you did. The sad part is that you'll continue to do this unless you do something radically different.

The Problem Isn't You

It's the way you've been taught to set goals. Hands down, the biggest player is the S.M.A.R.T. goal-setting system, but even if you're using one of the others, they're all missing a key ingredient. Do you ever wonder if that's why they're called "Goal Setting" systems" and not "Goal Getting" or "Goal Achievement" systems?

The missing ingredient makes achieving goals not just possible but inevitable. Without it, you're doomed to repeat the same tired cycle of frustration and disappointment year after year.

Imagine, instead, a system that virtually guarantees you'll follow through on your goals.

See yourself not just setting them but smashing them. Picture a life where you actually become the person you know you can be and do all the things you set out to do. Think of the pride you'll feel completing them all instead of the usual guilt when you quit three weeks into the year.

The best part? This book is going to show you how to do just that.

Why Will This System Work When Others Haven't?

Because it's based on what's proven to work. Through scientifically validated methods like accountability, specific planning, tracking resources, and more, this book will guide you through the process that ensures your success.

It's not wishful thinking. It's not theory — it's tested, and it works.

Even if you only take away the most crucial element (the one that's missing in all the other methods), it will change how you approach your goals forever.

This is not just another pseudo-scientific self-help book. It's your roadmap to achieving real, measurable results.

So, what's next? Turn the page. In the next chapter, I will show you exactly why the S.M.A.R.T. goal-setting system is doomed to fail, why it doesn't work, and why you've been stuck.

More importantly, I'll introduce you to the solution that will change everything — A.S.P.I.R.E.

WHY SMART GOALS DON'T WORK?

I f you've been paying attention and are self-employed, an entrepreneur, or involved in the corporate world, you've probably seen or heard of the ubiquitous S.M.A.R.T. acronym. It allegedly stands for

SPECIFIC,

MEASURABLE,

ATTAINABLE,

REALISTIC,

AND TIMELY.

(There are some other variants where "attainable" might be replaced with "achievable," and you might also see "time-bound" instead of timely.)

Likewise, if you've ever read even one of the many articles about setting New Year's resolutions that crop up every December, you've undoubtedly seen the term S.M.A.R.T. goals.

S.M.A.R.T. goals also appear in almost every self-help book and online course devoted to personal development and success.

Given how often you see it, it would seem America and the rest of the English-speaking world lack a viable alternative.

The authors of those articles, the corporate trainers, and the motivational speakers claim all you must do to achieve your goals is ensure they meet those S.M.A.R.T. requirements. If you do, you're good to go. The people who publish the journals and planners apparently believe the same thing.

I can't believe the S.M.A.R.T. goal system has existed for so long without anyone questioning its validity. I mean, come on. If a system doesn't work over ninety percent of the time, wouldn't you look for a better one?

If it were true, everyone who wrote out their resolutions would achieve them, every business would succeed in meeting their goals, and everyone else would be skinny and rich. Or am I missing something?

The best part about it is that nobody blames the S.M.A.R.T. goal system when it doesn't work. They end up blaming themselves.

I can't believe the S.M.A.R.T. goal system has existed for so long without anyone questioning its validity. I mean, come on. If a system doesn't work over ninety percent of the time, wouldn't you look for a better one?

If you study it, you'll quickly realize it's nothing more than a checklist. I bet you didn't know this. It has nothing to do with setting or achieving goals in its original form.

Where It Came From

George T. Doran, the gentleman credited with coming up with S.M.A.R.T., created it as a management objective checklist in November of 1981.

Doran was a consultant and was once a Director of Corporate Planning for the Washington Water Power Company. In its original form, the S stood for "Specific," the M for "measurable," the A for **"ASSIGNABLE,"** the R for "realistic," and the T for "time-related."

Management wasn't happy with the employee's performance, so they brought Mr. Doran in. After talking with the employees, he realized they weren't being given clear guidance by management.

As a result, George came up with the S.M.A.R.T. acronym.

He told management that before sending off your objectives to your underlings, you were supposed to run them through S.M.A.R.T. to ensure they covered all bases. Was the task specific? Check. Was it measurable? Check. Was it assignable? Check. (More on that in a minute.) Was it realistic? Check. Was it time-bound or timely? Check.

Initially, the A was never for "attainable" or "achievable." The human resource (HR) trainers and self-help gurus who hijacked the acronym decided it should be different. In the original version, the objective had to be assigned to someone, hence the A standing for assignable.

Goal setting is nothing.
Goal achievement is everything.

Somehow, somewhere along the line, the whole system, initially nothing more than a guideline for assigning work orders, got hijacked by people as a goal-setting system.

All they had to do was tweak the letter A, and bingo, they had their system's acronym. And boy, didn't it sound great. S.M.A.R.T.: What's not to love?

Unfortunately, as a goal achievement system, it sucks.

No Scientific Backing

To begin with, did you know no scientific studies have been done to back up S.M.A.R.T? In fact, a Harvard Business Review article on goal setting called it banal (Grote, 2017). Look at the statistics: only eight percent of people achieve their New Year's resolutions.

A Harvard Business Review article on goal setting called The SMART goal setting system BANAL (Grote, 2017)

Surely, with so many people touting this system, the numbers would be better than that. It would seem obvious it doesn't work. And yet, every year, every corporate event and every motivational speaker's goal-setting workshop begins with this overworked nonsense.

Okay, let's dig a little deeper, and I'll explain why S.M.A.R.T. is so useless.

The first thing you learn in goal setting is that general goals aren't any good. "Lose weight" will never work because it needs an amount and a time limit if it stands any chance of working. Why? Because otherwise, you'd lose an ounce, and your goal would be achieved.

Tony Robbins talks about the same thing. When he asks what your goal is and someone replies, *"To make more money,"* he tosses them a quarter and says, *"There you go, mission accomplished."*

Without a precise target, you can hit your goals all too easily and never arrive at where you really want to be.

The S.M.A.R.T. system recognizes this. The very first letter stands for Specific.

The problem is that the second you add the amount of weight or money or the time limit to make your goal specific, you have done away with the M and the T in the S.M.A.R.T. acronym. How did nobody catch this?

What Do I Mean?

If something is specific, wouldn't it already be measurable and timely? One appropriate definition of "specific" is *"stated explicitly or in detail."* So, while I have no problem with a goal being specific (and yes, they should be), the measurable and timely aspects of S.M.A.R.T. have now become redundant.

How else can you be specific without using the elements of measure and time? I would have been less critical of the system if the first letter had been a G for "General."

That way, your general goal would have been to "lose weight," "make more money," or "write a book," and then the M and the T would be appropriate.

That way, you could ask,

"How much weight exactly?

How much money precisely?" and

How long will the book be?" and then we'd want to implement a deadline.

G.M.A.R.T. doesn't sound nearly as cool as S.M.A.R.T., though, does it?

If you agree that both "measurable" and "timely" are now rendered obsolete, that leaves us with the acronym S.A.R. Your goal would now be specific, attainable, and realistic.

Uh oh. Houston, we have another problem. Aren't "attainable" and "realistic" the same thing? How could it possibly be one and not the other?

Is it realistic to be able to drop twenty pounds in one year? Yep, sure it is. Then, isn't that automatically attainable? Is it realistic to be able to quit smoking? Yes. Isn't it achievable, then?

If you're a proponent of the system, please tell me a goal that's realistic but not achievable. I'll wait.

Conversely, tell me about your goal that's definitely achievable but not realistic.

That means we have to do away with either attainable or realistic. Now, your goal would be specific and realistic or specific and attainable.

In a nutshell, that means "measurable" and "timely" are redundant, and you only need "attainable" OR "realistic" but not both. That leaves you with S for "specific" and A for "attainable." Spelled backward, that's AS, as in, "as much use as a chocolate fireman."

To hammer home the point, let's look at a goal of losing weight using S.M.A.R.T., and then let's look at the same goal using SA.

First with S.M.A.R.T.:

SPECIFIC: I want to lose 20lbs by the first of Jan

MEASURE: 20lbs (redundant)

ACHIEVABLE: Yes

REALISTIC: Yes (redundant)

TIME BOUND: First of Jan. (redundant)

And now, with SA

SPECIFIC: I want to lose 20lbs by the 1st of Jan

ACHIEVABLE: Yes.

Another problem with S.M.A.R.T. goals is that very little of it is scientifically proven. There has been much research on what constitutes practical goal setting, and S.M.A.R.T. goals don't figure into the equation.

The biggest revelation from all that research on achieving goals was that money or one's reputation should be involved to increase the chance of success. Just where are money and reputation in S.M.A.R.T?

Dr. Dean Karlan, Professor of Behavioral Economics at Yale University, found that people tripled their chance of success if one of two things were involved: either they paid money if they didn't achieve their intended goal or if their reputation was on the line.

Please read that again. People tripled their chance of success if they had to pay money if they failed or if their reputation was on the line.

Where is that in S.M.A.R.T.? There's zero mention of money being involved, and there's no mention of reputation being involved. (F.Y.I., they're both forms of accountability. More on that soon.)

Most scientifically validated research concerning goals has no mention in S.M.A.R.T. other than they should be specific if they stand any chance of being done.

A Better Way

After failing to achieve many of the annual goals I'd set by following S.M.A.R.T., I decided there had to be a better way. I started researching using my antecedents in martial arts and the military and checking out what the scientists interested in this field were doing. Then, I came up with an altogether different acronym utilizing all the available research that suddenly saw me making leaps and bounds in achieving my goals.

It didn't matter whether they were financial, personal, career, accomplishment, family, or spiritual goals.

This new way of looking at goal setting worked faster and better than any other system I've used from the myriad of books I've read on the subject over the years. Once again, it's all scientifically validated.

The acronym is A.S.P.I.R.E.

Not only does it come from the word "Aspiration," which means "A strong desire for high achievement, or to achieve something, such as success," but each aspect of it is based on the latest goal-setting research done by scientists and behavioral psychologists.

Read the next chapter to learn all about the most critical element of all.

KEY POINTS

- If a goal is specific, it HAS to have a measure and a time limit.

- M & T in the S.M.A.R.T. acronym are redundant.

- A goal can't be attainable and not realistic, and vice versa.

- Nothing in S.M.A.R.T. has ever been scientifically validated or researched.

THE MISSING INGREDIENT

In this chapter, you will learn about the missing ingredient in the S.M.A.R.T. system. Without this particular ingredient, you will forever remain one of the 92% who set goals but never achieve them.

It's the only thing that ensures the average person gets things done, especially when they don't want to or they lack sufficient motivation.

It's called ACCOUNTABILITY.

I want you to think for a moment about all the things that get done that people don't want to do.

Most children, for example, only clean their rooms, eat their vegetables, and do their homework because their parents hold them accountable. *"If you don't clean your room, you're not having dessert." "You are not leaving this table until you've eaten everything on your plate." "You cannot play outside until you've shown me your homework."*

In some families, mine included, that accountability included spanking or some form of corporal punishment. Your allowance, or pocket money, was doled out only if your chores had been done. Desserts and TV privileges were withheld to force compliance.

Accountability was also an integral part of many schools. You learned very quickly about consequences. If you didn't do your homework, there would be hell to pay. If you talked out of turn in class, you might be sent to detention or made to write something a thousand times. Committing a serious enough offense would mean being caned. (I understand the US equivalent is called "paddling").

Every kid I went to school with called it double trouble. The teacher would catch us doing something wrong. Depending on the teacher, he might throw a piece of chalk, an eraser, or come down and yank you out of your seat by the hair. He'd then send us to the principal's office, where we'd be caned.

Next, the headmaster or principal would phone your parents. You came home to a mother who sent you to your room without a snack or being allowed outside to play. You sat there awaiting the arrival of your father. Most times, more punishment ensued, hence the double trouble moniker.

Not Just for Kids

How about adults in the workforce? Do you arrive on time to work? Most employees do, not because they're self-disciplined or self-aware, but because their boss or manager is taking notes, and there will be consequences if they don't.

Do you finish your work, return right after lunch, stay till quitting time, and dress per your employer's dress code? You probably do. And why? Again, because someone is holding you accountable.

Do you register your vehicle, wear a seat belt, obey the speed limit, stop at red lights, and not drive drunk? Again, most of us do it because a police officer or a camera is watching, and the enforcement machine is holding us accountable.

What about paying taxes, getting a passport before you travel overseas, not putting weapons in your carry-on when you fly, etc.? Again, in this instance, the Feds are holding you accountable.

Whether in our homes as kids, in school, at work as adults, or out in the world as responsible citizens, a lot of what we do only happens because we're being held accountable.

By the way, if you are one of those rare few who, as a child, without being told, cleaned your room, ate your vegetables, did your homework, and got up without hitting the snooze button and who, as an adult, consistently achieve your New Year's resolutions, meet all your deadlines, arrive at work on time, leave late, do your job and then some, obey all speed limits and road signs because it's the right thing to do, then congratulations.

You can probably safely put this book down (give it to one of your less disciplined friends) because I doubt you'll need it. You are almost certainly one of the eight percent who don't need to be held accountable.

For the rest of us, ordinary mere mortals, people who need someone looking over our shoulders and who need to be held responsible for our work and behavior, getting things done, and being appropriate, read on.

Why on earth would anyone think, believe, or even agree with the idea that if I simply write down, "I want to have a net worth of $500,000 in five years" or, "I will lose twenty-five pounds by Christmas," that it's going to happen?

Why would it happen just because you wrote it down?

Take the twenty-five-pound weight loss by July goal, for example.

It's specific, it's got a measure, it's attainable, it's realistic, and it's got a time frame. So, according to the proponents of the S.M.A.R.T. goal system, you should lose the weight.

So why doesn't it happen?

To begin with, there's nothing about the discipline necessary to stop eating junk food. Nor is there any mention of the discipline needed to go and do the required exercises.

Most importantly, there's no accountability. Where's that? That's the most essential piece of the puzzle. Without that crucial element, the goal could only work under two circumstances: you are a self-disciplined tour de force, or someone is making you.

How about some other typical goals I see bandied about every year? What about any financial goals you set or your plan to write a book?

I will save $5,000 by Christmas or write a 300-page book on underwater basket weaving by next March. Again, are you seriously telling me they'll get done just because you wrote them down on a list?

And yet, both goals are specific, measurable, attainable, realistic, and timely. They meet every requirement as per the S.M.A.R.T. system.

Again, without a ton of self-discipline or someone holding you accountable, you have very little chance of achieving either. This is why we get discouraged, beat ourselves up, and consider ourselves failures repeatedly.

Well, the good news is it's not your fault at all. You've simply been following the wrong plan. Do you realize that if someone had held you accountable, you would have accomplished all of them?

Does that mean it will be easy? Nope. No way. It will be hard, and the more audacious the goal, the harder it will be. But the big difference is what you actually accomplish.

Without the accountability factor, you'll have a list of wishes you add to your calendar every year. Sure, they'll feel good when you write them down, but they'll depress you when you pull them out next year and realize you didn't complete one of them.

However, you'll experience an entirely different outcome with the accountability factor at play. You'll be able to proudly look at a list of accomplishments that are all checked off. You'll have moved ahead and be ready to write out next year's goals, secure in the knowledge that they, too, will get done.

If you're not convinced that accountability is the missing ingredient, consider the following:

To quit smoking is undoubtedly challenging. Everyone knows it. Millions of people every year try to stop the demon nicotine and, sure as a bullfrog is waterproof, every year they fail and light right back up.

Accountability Vs. Smart

Now, let's compare the two systems. S.M.A.R.T. goals with zero accountability and the method that includes being held accountable. Be warned, I will use an extreme example of accountability for illustration purposes only.

S.M.A.R.T. goal adherents write down, "I will stop smoking my pack a day starting tomorrow and never take it up again. According to the proponents of the system, they check every box. They've got a specific goal, i.e., he will quit smoking cigarettes tomorrow. His measure is his pack a day. It's attainable, realistic, and time-bound.

I submit you need to be held accountable if you want to guarantee the outcome. So, while they're doing that, I'll get someone who wants to quit, who claims he can't. I'll walk around behind that person twenty-four/seven with a shotgun with the promise that, if a cigarette even touches their lips, I'll pull the trigger. I know it's an extreme example, but bear with me.

Would you put any money on the guy following the S.M.A.R.T. system?

Whereas, I'd be willing to bet you a million dollars that my guy wouldn't smoke. "I can't quit" is complete rubbish if you're properly motivated and being held accountable by someone. Guess when drug addicts hooked on heroin or crack quit cold turkey. Most times, it's when they go to prison.

Where there is no vision,

the people perish

Proverbs 29:18

So, where exactly is the accountability in S.M.A.R.T.? It's not there. That's why it so rarely works. You've been beating yourself up all this time, thinking something must be wrong because you never see anything through.

The problem doesn't lie with you. It never did. It lies with the fact that all the gurus, corporate trainers, H.R. people, and authors of the ubiquitous New Year's Resolution articles failed to mention that your goals stand very little chance of being accomplished without accountability.

Remember what Karlan said. "People tripled their chance of success if one of two things were involved: either they paid money if they didn't achieve their intended goal or if their reputation was on the line."

They're both forms of accountability, aren't they?

Yes, S.M.A.R.T. is an okay checklist if all you want to do is SET goals. (It's not, but we'll cover that in subsequent chapters). It's a wretched system if you wish to ACHIEVE your goals.

So, now you know what doesn't work, let's get on with learning the system that does work. The system that's scientifically validated. The one that's not so much about goal setting as it is about goal achieving.

KEY POINTS

- 92% of people fail to achieve their goals every year.
- New Year's resolutions are often given up before the end of January.
- S.M.A.R.T. doesn't work (if it did, everyone would be skinny and rich).
- S.M.A.R.T. has zero scientific research.
- Without accountability, nothing gets done.

ACCOUNTABILITY

I n this chapter, you will learn how to implement the missing ingredient we discussed in the previous chapter.

The acronym A.S.P.I.R.E. starts with the letter A. That A stands for "Accountable." The dictionary defines this as "the state of being accountable; liability to be called on to render an account; accountableness responsible for; answerable for."

Irrefutably, this is the most critical aspect of setting one's goal and achieving it, which is why it is first place in the acronym.

This is the one I meant when I said earlier that even if you only took one aspect of this book, it would change your success rate with goal accomplishment most dramatically.

It is missing in almost all goal-setting courses, diet books, get-rich plans, and everything else in the self-improvement/self-help genre.

You can apply this one aspect to any self-help books gathering dust on your shelves that didn't work, and the stuff inside will work just fine. You can incorporate it with your New Year's resolutions, and they'll probably get done for the first time in your life. That's especially true if you're like most people who, we've learned, quit their resolutions by January 20th of each year.

Accountability Works

Accountability is why we all got up and ran fifteen kilometers every morning in the Foreign Legion. It wasn't because we, as individuals, were motivated. It was because we were held accountable by our NCOs, who were, in turn, held accountable by their superior officers all the way up the food chain, including our generals and their bosses in the French Ministry of Defense.

Why do projects get done in corporate America? Because someone, somewhere, is looking over the team's shoulder, making sure the work gets done, and if it doesn't, heads will roll.

Why don't you drive 140 mph down the highway? Why don't you drive without a seatbelt? Why don't you drive home drunk? Why don't you get out of your car and go ballistic on the guy who just cut you off and nearly caused you to have a serious accident? Why do you get out of bed in the morning and go to work instead of sleeping in until noon? Why do you pay taxes?

The simple answer to all the above is accountability. Society, your family, law enforcement, and the government, amongst others, are all holding you accountable. If you don't file your taxes, or you get caught driving drunk, etc., then there will be, in no uncertain terms, hell to pay.

As you learned earlier, you give me someone who claims they can't quit smoking, and I could make them stop in a heartbeat. I apologize again for the extreme example, but let me hold a gun on them, with the promise that if they light up, I will pull the trigger.

There's no way they will succumb to that allegedly irresistible craving. I want to make the point that almost every goal that doesn't get accomplished fails due to a lack of accountability or willpower and not much else.

Accountability kicks in when willpower wanes. It doesn't matter how much willpower someone has, either. When they reach that point where they can't possibly go on, and someone or something holds them accountable, you can bet they'll find it within themselves to keep going.

We learned in the Legion that a horse will run till its lungs burst, whereas a man will give you about forty percent of what he's capable of and tell you he's done. Interestingly enough, the renowned David Goggins of Navy SEAL and ultra-marathon fame mentioned the same percentage in his book "Can't Hurt Me."

When I worked with my self-employed friends and clients, I was their "Accountability Coach." They, being self-employed, didn't have anyone looking over their shoulders, unlike their counterparts working for a boss.

That makes it very easy to waste time and not get the work done that needs doing. That's where I came into the picture. I was the guy who held their feet to the fire and made sure their deadlines were met. As a result, their productivity went through the roof. The instant their output was monitored, it doubled and tripled almost without fail.

Once again, it doesn't matter where you look. The stuff nobody wants to do gets done because someone is holding someone accountable for it.

As previously mentioned, the guys at Yale who discovered that goals were three times more likely to be achieved if money or reputation were on the line launched a fantastic website called Stickk.com, where members of the public can pledge money to other people to ensure their goals are achieved.

"It is not only what we do, but also

what we do not do, for which

we are accountable."

- *Moliere.*

This is huge. This is the missing ingredient. This is why everyone isn't skinny, happy, and rich. This is why self-help books haven't done much to date unless the reader already has a fantastic amount of willpower and determination all on his own.

How Serious Are You?

I had dinner with friends of mine a few years ago and told them about writing this book. One of them, Carey, had a goal to quit smoking, so I told her about the accountability aspect of my goal-setting acronym. I suggested she write a check for three thousand dollars that I'd cash if she didn't stay off the cigarettes. She balked at the idea of writing the check. That told me all I needed to know about how serious her goal was to quit smoking. (Sadly, I heard she had a stroke a few years ago as a result of her smoking habit) If she'd written the check, I'd submit that she would have stuck to the goal.

This form of accountability, i.e., pledging money, will immediately confirm how serious you are about your goals. When it comes time to put pen to paper and write a check (or however you want to transfer the money) for a significant amount and put that money on the line, dependent on your willingness to follow through, you begin to discover what goals are important and which are nothing but pie in the sky.

With all due respect to Dr. Karlan and his team at Yale, I've taken the accountability factor one step further.

My problem with pledging to random people or charities, etc., is that there's not enough pressure to get things done. When you get to that tipping point of "if I don't do this, the money goes," it's not enough if it goes to just anyone.

So, here's my method of being held accountable, which nobody else, as far as I know, uses. Watch how it gets done if you're dead serious about achieving a particular goal.

Significance

Firstly, whether you decide to write a check, timebomb the money in a payment app, or have the funds held in escrow, make the amount significant enough that, while you can pay it, it will cause you considerable pain to part with.

Seriously. For this to work, it has to be enough money to give you pause. (Sometimes we make two amounts, but more on that in a bit)

Now, and this is key to the whole system: make the beneficiary someone or some organization you absolutely cannot stand. You have to despise them. Once you've decided who that is, give the money to your accountability partner to send if you don't complete your assigned task.

We'll go into this more later in the book, but obviously, your accountability partner has to be someone who's going to hold you accountable. I recommend not using your significant other, a family member, or a friend.

If you're going to get mad with them for sticking to their guns and forwarding your money if you get off track, you don't want it to cause a rift. Similarly, don't pick someone who will cave in and give the money back the second you start whining when the going gets tough. That defeats the entire system.

Abhorrence

What do I mean by making the money payable to a person or organization you hate? If you're a die-hard Republican, make your check out to the "Re-elect the Democratics's Choice fund." Are you a died-in-the-wool, hard-core Democrat? Make yours go to the fund to elect the "Republican's Candidate for President."

Are you a Southern Baptist? Make yours to the local strip club or liquor store. Are you a Muslim fanatic? Make yours to Israel. Are you Israeli? Hezbollah is always looking for donations. Do you have an in-law or a sibling you can't stand the sight of? Is there someone at work who gets under your skin? You get the idea. How about your ex? Pick someone or some entity you absolutely cannot stand and make them the beneficiary.

Seriously. On a scale of 1 to 10, what are your chances of failure now? Given the ends you'll go to ensure your nemesis doesn't get your hard-earned money, I'd submit almost zero.

This concept of accountability alone, the missing ingredient, is enough to ensure you'll achieve your aims without benefiting from the other aspects of A.S.P.I.R.E. However, with the different elements, you'll have the tools to make this a cakewalk.

I'm aware of two women who have a goal to keep their weight down to a certain level. Tony Robbins talks about them on several of his programs. Both women have a can of dog food sitting on their refrigerator and agree that, at the end of the year, should they be over their desired weight, they have to eat the dog food. So far, they're still on track, and no doubt, seeing the can every time they go near the fridge and thinking about the possibility of having to eat the contents is what's working to keep them in line.

The Two Amounts Method

I said I'd mention the concept of two amounts of money earlier on. I got this from my friend A.J. Puedan of Success Coach Technologies.

Depending on your goal, sometimes it will benefit you to set up two payments. The first one is for an amount of money that will hurt, as mentioned above. The second amount is more significant and substantial enough that it's really going to hurt—got it?

The first one hurts.

The second one really hurts.

The amount of money will obviously depend on your financial circumstances.

Someone like Oprah or Warren Buffett will write checks out for far more significant amounts than someone currently out of work. Just so long as the amounts do what they're supposed to do, i.e., hurt, then really hurt, that's all that matters.

"Life is not accountable to us. We are accountable to life." - Denis Waitley

A Shot Across the Bow

Now, the first amount, regardless of whether it's a check, money order, cash timebomb in a financial app, or being held in escrow, is used as a shot across the bows. A warning of what will happen next if you don't do what you've said you would.

Let's use losing weight as an example. At the start of the year, you've decided to lose thirty pounds by December. June rolls around, and you haven't done anything about achieving that goal. You haven't bought a diet book. You haven't thrown out the candy and junk food in the house. You haven't stopped eating fast food. You haven't begun an exercise program. You haven't contacted a personal trainer or even joined a gym. You climb on the scales in front of your accountability partner, and indeed, you're a couple of pounds heavier than when you weighed yourself at the start of the year.

This is where your accountability partner, henceforth known as your AP, sends off the smaller of the two amounts. This is the shot across the bows to prove that your goal and your AP are serious.

Your money will go to someone or some organization you cannot stand. If you continue on your current course of action, the 2nd, more significant amount will go next. We're not playing around. This method will guarantee it gets done if it absolutely must be done. Of course, if you're going to be a weakling about it and cry like a little girl when they threaten to send it, then stop now and go back to your old favorite method that doesn't work.

I use this two-amount method because that's what we respond best to. Think about the legal system. You usually get a warning ticket the first time you commit an infraction. The second time, you get a fine. Next, you get a more significant fine, and eventually, you get a custodial sentence.

The home I grew up in was the same. The first time I did something wrong, I'd get admonished, but if I kept it up, the punishments became harsher.

Proof

Let me prove a point about the efficacy of making the money amount to someone you despise and not just a friend, a stranger, or a charity. At the Grant Cardone Growth Conference in Las Vegas in 2018, I told the guy beside me about my system. He told me, ruefully, that he wished he'd met me earlier.

He'd signed up to be coached by one of Grant Cardone's coaches. Apparently, Grant has the same idea about using money to ensure your goals are met. My seatmate had paid a lot of money to one of Grant's coaches and pledged the money to his charity of choice to make sure the homework he was assigned was done.

He confessed to me that he didn't do the work, but he didn't mind because his charity got the money, which was a tax write-off.

With all due respect to Grant's guys, that will never work as an incentive. My seminar mate weighed the pain of doing his homework versus the pain of a check going to his favorite charity and getting a write-off. Of course, the work didn't get done. Imagine if, instead of his charity, it was someone he hated, perhaps his competition in the town where he lived. I'd wager whatever you like, his homework would have been completed. He, at least, agreed it would have.

Okay, so before we go onto the next chapter, where you will learn what the letter S stands for and why it's critical to this system, just think about who your accountability partner will be.

I'm going to repeat it. Based on experience, I advise you not to use a friend or family member, or anyone you will burn bridges with if they do their job regarding the accountability factor.

It's too easy for this to ruin friendships and relationships. They will either be guilted by you into not sending the money or risk alienating you by doing what they signed up for.

You want someone who will do what's required and who won't give a damn if you start complaining or trying to renege on your half of the deal. It's a tall order, so choose well. You might also want to consider having a contract drawn up so there's no he said/she said as the deadline for sending the money nears. (I'll put one on my www.NickHughesCoaching.com resource page)

You might also consider getting a coach. That's one of the things I did for my clients. They unequivocally knew I wouldn't cave if I had to send the money. It's called tough love, and it's what they paid me for.

KEY POINTS

- Accountability is the main reason stuff gets done.
- Few self-employed people have someone holding them accountable.
- Scientific research shows that money and reputation are why goals are accomplished.
- Money and reputation are forms of accountability.
- Make the money pledge to someone or thing you loathe to be genuinely effective.
- Ensure your accountability partner is not someone you'll be upset with if the friendship or relationship is ruined.
- Equally, ensure your AP will stick to their guns and send the money no matter what excuses you try to use if you don't accomplish your goal.
- Consider drawing up a contract to make the pledge legally binding.

SHARED/SPECIFIC

The S in ASPIRE has two meanings. The first S stands for **"Shared."** Like accountability, this is another crucial and scientifically proven step to achieving your goals. The second S stands for **"Specific."** Likewise, this is also critical.

Remember, Dr. Karlan's finding at Yale was if a man's money or reputation is on the line, he's three times more likely to see his goal through.

The "accountability" step of A.S.P.I.R.E. takes care of the money aspect. In other words, you're staking an amount of money that will go to someone you don't like if you don't accomplish your goal.

Sharing

Sharing your goal takes care of the reputation side of the equation. Think about it for a moment. If you wake up on January 1 intending to stop smoking, join the gym, or run a marathon, and you don't tell anyone, what's to prevent you from quitting?

41

Nobody is going to know. Sure, you'll feel guilty when you light up a cigarette on the second of January or quit going to the gym by week three. You'll no doubt indulge in some negative self-talk after you give up your marathon training program the first time it starts to hurt. If not negative self-talk, you can always fall back on your lame justifications. "I'm too busy," "I'll start next week," "Smoking isn't that bad," "So what if I don't? Lots of people are overweight."

Don't worry, you're not alone. Millions of people wake up on January 1 of every year with all sorts of grandiose plans to conquer the world, and yet, surveys show that only a dismal eight percent will see their goals through to completion. According to the same surveys, the ninety-two percent that quit will throw in the towel by January 20!!! Not even three weeks into the year. Wow!

Sharing your goals, on the other hand, changes that. What if, instead of keeping these things to yourself – and let's face it, many people do that on purpose – you tell your family, friends, and co-workers about your plans? You now have two groups of people who will help you stay on track, depending on what type of motivation you respond to.

Your Support Team

The first group will be those who offer you support and encouragement. Whether from your immediate family or friends, they'll be your fan club and cheerleaders, providing a gentle push when the going gets tough. For many of you, maybe it will only be your mother, but there'll always be at least one person who falls into this cheerleader camp.

Your Detractors

The second group will be those who will tease and mock you about your attempts and try to de-rail you. It might be a jealous sibling or co-worker. Perhaps it's a friend who can't quit smoking, who doesn't want to see you succeed because it's going to make him feel worse about himself. You're shining a spotlight on his weakness and inability to quit.

Maybe it's your overweight couch potato friend who's now going to feel guilty as you get into shape and begin to see your goal through. Perhaps it's a co-worker who feels belittled because you plan to follow your entrepreneurial dream and open your own business.

"There are two ways to have the biggest building. Build the biggest building or knock everyone else's down." Jim Rohn

It doesn't matter what their motivation is. You know they're out there and will do everything they can to pull you down to their level. They're a lot like the famous crabs in the bucket. They can't stand it whenever someone looks like they're going to better themselves. They'll do everything in their power to try and drag you back down to make themselves feel better. What did Jim Rohn used to say? *"There are two ways to have the biggest building. Build the biggest building or knock everyone else's down."*

I don't know about you, but the latter group is the one I respond to best. Some people need encouragement and cheerleaders. Others, like me, respond better to the naysayers and rise to the challenge at the laying down of the gauntlet. I love nothing better than proving those people wrong.

Patrick Bet David, an Iranian entrepreneur, wrote a book entitled "**Choose Your Enemies Wisely.**" In it, he talks about the attack on his father by family and friends and how it inspired him to go from being a wastrel to becoming a multi-millionaire business owner. (FYI, the book is excellent, and if you haven't read it yet, you should)

Doctors told me after I had Osteomyelitis[1] as a kid that sports were out and I'd be lucky to walk again. I went on to play Rugby, Judo, and boxing and compete in full-contact karate. At one time, I was ranked the youngest fifth-degree black belt in the world. When I told others I planned to take off and join the French Foreign Legion to pursue my dream of being a bodyguard, a slew of them told me I was crazy and that it would never happen.

In the Legion, they told me I was too big to join the parachute regiment, which I did anyway. According to my friends, there were women and models I was crazy to try and date since they were out of my league, and then I was told I was mad to try and set up my own business.

"Keep your fears to yourself, but share your inspiration with others."
- Robert Louis Stevenson.

---

[1] Osteomyelitis is a disease that infects the marrow of the bone and can potentially kill you. I contracted it when I was young and had my last rites read several times during my hospital stay.

Perhaps my favorite naysayer comment was about the building I bought and sold a few months after opening my first business in the US. I had initially moved my business into the bottom floor of a building in a rundown part of town.

When the real estate boom hit, that particular area went through gentrification, and property values started jumping. I wanted to buy the building and, because I'd been such an exemplary tenant (I spent a lot of money fixing the building up even though it belonged to my landlady and I would never usually get a penny of that money back), my landlady gave me first shot at it.

Unfortunately, I had trouble qualifying for a loan because I lived upstairs, and the business was downstairs. Unlike many cities where that's relatively common, this was an anomaly. When the residential loan people heard the company was downstairs, they said I needed a commercial loan. When the commercial loan people heard I lived upstairs, they said I needed a residential loan.

At this point, everybody tried to talk me out of buying. After six months and a lot of money spent on appraisals, being ripped off by a bank, and running into many dead ends, I didn't have a single person in the cheerleading camp, including my spouse (now my ex). They all kept telling me, "It's just not meant to be.

You need to quit." The more they told me I couldn't do it, the more determined I became to prove them wrong.

I even went back to school to get my real estate license to try and find a loophole in the laws and regulations, which is precisely what happened. I discovered something called a property purchase mortgage and was able to buy the building after negotiating some other hurdles with both the banks and the landlady. I purchased the building, put some money into cosmetic repairs, and, six months later, accepted an offer for roughly four times what I'd paid for it.

Perseverance paid off, but more importantly, so did my crew in the *"it'll never happen, why don't you just accept it and move on"* crowd. Without them, I probably would have given up, but, being the obstinate jackass that I am, I had no choice but to prove them all wrong.

Don't worry about it if you respond better to the encouragement. There's nothing wrong with that approach either, and the beauty of it is that it will be a two-pronged approach based on human nature.

Some people you share with will tell you, *"That's great,"* and others will try and tell you you're mad for trying. Use whichever one you need to fire yourself up, and get it done.

Social Media Makes It Easy

One of the most significant advantages you have, by the way, regarding sharing your goals is the internet. In the old days, the only people likely to find out about your plans would have been your immediate family, friends, and co-workers. Nowadays, we have the website stickk.com, where you can go on and declare your intentions to the world, but even better is the ubiquitous Facebook™ and all the other forms of social media.

I keep waiting for Facebook to develop a goals tab where you can post your intentions. That way, your friends could check in on them and see if you're on target or not. How simple is that? You go on and declare to everyone on your friend's list that you are planning to run your marathon, lose weight, quit smoking, go back to school, open a business, get your black belt, ride your bike around America, write your first novel, hike the Appalachian trail, climb Mt. Everest, or all of the above. Within a few hours, all your people will be holding you accountable, including your cheer squad, detractors, and naysayers. Absolutely brilliant.

SPECIFIC

So, onto SPECIFIC. If you're into personal development, or you've heard of or used S.M.A.R.T. goals before, you know the S stands for "Specific." As much as I despise the S.M.A.R.T. acronym for the reasons stated in the chapter on "Why S.M.A.R.T. Goals Are Dumb," they're right about specificity.

Car manufacturers don't say, "We need to build more cars next year." They know precisely how many, what colors, what models, and which part of the country they will ship to.

How about the old saw from the self-help industry as to why this is important? Tony Robbins says it all the time. If someone has a goal of *"I want to make more money,"* you give them a dollar and say, *"Mission accomplished."*

How about people trying to lose weight? I've lost count of the number of friends of mine over the years who've told me, *"I need to lose some weight"* or, *"God, I jumped on the scales the other day. I really need to lose a few pounds."*

Whether it's the money, the weight, or something else, if your subconscious mind has a goal and it's achieved, it will now switch off regarding that goal. So, when you say, *"I want more money,"* and you find a five-dollar note in your coat pocket, the subconscious assumes, *"Mission accomplished."*

Likewise, if you say, *"I need to lose some weight,"* and you weigh a pound less the next time you're on the scales, you're done as far as your subconscious is concerned.

So, whatever your goal is, remember to be absolutely specific. Merriam-Webster defines that as *"free from ambiguity: Accurate."*

Here are some examples to give you the idea:

"I intend to retire with a net worth of $2,400,000 on September 25th, 2033. The money will come from a combination of work, side hustles, savvy investing, and leveraged income from online courses I will create.

"I will drop 15lbs by the 15th of December 2025. I will use a combination of cleaning up my diet, intermittent fasting, and working out three days a week.

"I will join a running club by the end of next month and run a marathon in under 4 hours within exactly eight months of joining the club."

"I will call precisely 20 clients and potential clients every Monday to Friday before I leave the office for lunch each day. If I don't get the person on the phone, they won't count towards my list of twenty."

I'm sure you get the idea. Whether it's a family goal, a career goal, financial or fun, it must be specific if you want your subconscious to go to work for you and make it happen.

"If you don't know where you're going, you'll end up someplace else." -Yogi Berra

KEY POINTS

- Goals must be shared otherwise, nobody will know if you give up.
- People will be divided into two camps: those who encourage and those who belittle you.
- Everyone responds best to one of the above two types.
- Social media makes the sharing of goals easy.
- Websites like Stickk.com help with accountability.
- Goals must be specific if they're going to work.
- The more details you include in your definition, the better it will be for your subconscious to go to work.

PLANNED

The next step in the A.S.P.I.R.E. acronym is the letter P, which stands for **"Planned."** As the famous motivational speaker Zig Ziglar used to say, *"People do not wander around and then find themselves at the top of Mount Everest."*

Your goals must be planned and broken down into sub-goals or smaller steps. This is precisely the way it works in the military. You don't just name an operation and send a bunch of guys off to fight it. You figure out your objective, i.e., capture an enemy combatant to get information on troop strength, blow up a bridge, take a town, rescue some hostages, or invade a country. Once you've determined that, you figure out what you'll need to get the job done.

Will you use helicopters, planes, or trucks, or will you go on foot? Will you use a small squad of eight guys, a section, a company, a regiment, or your entire military? What weapons will they need to get the job done? Remember, the target always determines the weapon and not the other way around! How will troops get re-supplied? How will they know when the mission is done? How will you get them back home after it's over? You get the idea. Goals, objectives, missions, whatever you call them, must be planned.

Let's say you aim to run a marathon later this year. You don't just go out and start running twenty-six miles tomorrow morning. To do so would be stupid. Not only would it be physically detrimental, but you'd be so sore that you'd discourage yourself from ever running again. You'd be one of those ninety-two percent who quit by the third week of January.

Reverse Engineering

Instead, you'd break it down into a series of sub-goals and more than likely use the concept of reverse engineering. If it's January, for example, and the marathon is in October, you'd need to be comfortable running between eighteen to twenty miles by September. That means fifteen to eighteen miles in August and twelve to fifteen in July. Twelve to fifteen in July would mean ten to twelve in June and, more than likely, eight to ten in May, five to eight in April, four to five in March, two to three in February, and half a mile to a mile in January.

In some instances, you can figure out sub-goals by yourself; in others, there are books you can buy where someone has already done the work for you. You'd also have sub-goals of buying training shoes, a training journal, some books on training for a marathon, joining a running club, finding a partner, etc.

We break the study of martial arts down the same way. The goal for most adherents is a black belt, but there are sub-goals of yellow, orange, green, blue, and brown belts before reaching the black belt. It's no different with military ranks and titles in corporate America.

The other great thing about this planning phase is it breaks the goal down into incremental baby steps. Standing at the foot of a mountain, looking up at the peak, and seeing how far away it is can be daunting for anyone. If you look at the first ledge, however, maybe that's only fifteen feet away, and suddenly, it doesn't seem nearly as monumental a task. What's the old saying? You eat an elephant one bite at a time.

Many people set a goal of having a net worth of a million dollars. Very few achieve it, though, because they don't break down their goals realistically. It's not that hard. Using our reverse engineering example above of the marathon, how much would you have to have in year six if you want a net worth of a million dollars seven years from now? How much would you need in year five and so on? Drag out some paper, crunch the numbers, and then make your sub-goals accordingly.

"If you don't have daily objectives, you qualify as a dreamer." Zig Ziglar

It doesn't matter if your goal is long-term or only short-term. (I don't have any that go beyond ten years) Work it backward and figure out what you'll need every step of the way.

Of course, you can't break down every goal like this. For example, if your goal is to quit smoking, you can't reverse engineer it. Either you quit or you don't, but you can still break it down into sub-goals. Concerning quitting smoking, maybe you find an accountability partner and pledge the money, then read a book and do some online research on the most effective quitting methods. Maybe you're going to try hypnosis or a patch. Perhaps your doctor can advise you on the technique that uses an injection, or maybe you're just going to do it cold turkey. Lay them out in a logical sequence and get started.

There are many different ways to plan, and the problem is that none will apply in every situation. What works for the General trying to get troops out to fight WWIII in the Middle East might be somewhat different from what an aspiring entrepreneur might use to set up his new business. As previously mentioned, reverse engineering can work very well, but in our example of quitting smoking, it doesn't work well at all.

Start With Why

Before starting with your objective, consider your reason for wanting the goal. The "why" will usually give you the "how," and the how can be broken down into people, resources, equipment, etc. Also, considering potential obstacles or hurdles can help. Include any deadlines, such as an overseas trip that might require getting various shots for things like typhoid and cholera, and then put it all logically or chronologically. Begin checking them off as you do them.

"Our goals can only be reached through a vehicle of a plan, in which we must fervently believe and upon which we must vigorously act. There is no other route to success."

– Pablo Picasso.

You get the idea. It doesn't have to be anything fancy. You're not the General in charge of getting the entire Foreign Legion out to Iraq to participate in Desert Shield (though you can bet he had a plan that was broken down into smaller bite-sized chunks). Just keep it simple, and don't forget to leave a space for some rewards. (More on rewards in a minute.)

Types of Goals

The beauty of planning is that it lends itself to learning the process. We have several different types of goals, so distinguishing between them is essential. One type, for example, is a habit or process goal such as, "I'm going to meditate every day" or, "I'm going to spend time with my children," or "I'll go on a date night once a week with my significant other."

Another type of goal is an outcome goal. For an individual, that might be, "I will lose 30 pounds by Christmas," or "I will buy my Rolex Submariner on my birthday," or "I will run a marathon next year."

For a corporation, it could be a team goal of hitting so many projects completed by the end of the fiscal year or, for a sales representative working under a manager, clearing a certain financial amount.

Process V Outcome

Do you get the idea? The problem with outcome goals is that if we don't achieve them, we end up beating ourselves up, which can affect our self-esteem or self-worth. It doesn't even matter if you came close and achieved something epic. You can still label yourself a failure. How about a car salesman who aims to sell twenty cars next month? He sells eighteen, which is excellent, but he didn't hit twenty, so he considers himself a failure.

What if he set a process goal instead of setting an outcome goal? What's the process for selling a bunch of cars? He might want to participate in a sales course and read two books a month on being a better salesman. He might call twenty former clients daily and write thank you notes to every client requesting referrals. He might plan to greet every potential client driving onto the lot within sixty seconds of them getting out of the car.

His accountability partner still holds him accountable for following the process, but when he gets to the end of the month and sells eighteen vehicles, at least he stuck to the process. It's a win-win because now he's not beating himself up over missing an outcome.

Let's use a few more examples. How about the goal of writing a book? Trust me. It's daunting. How many potential authors have half-written manuscripts on their computers? They've given up and, as a result, are beating themselves up over failing to achieve an outcome? What if, instead, they got an accountability partner to ensure they stick to the process of writing a certain number of words per day?

A friend who'd published several books got me on track when he said, *"You sit in front of the computer every single morning, coffee in hand, and you don't leave till you've written three pages."* Other authors set targets of a certain number of words. Again, whatever method you use is irrelevant. Now, at the end of the year, if you've stuck to the process, you may not have gotten your book done, but you won't be beating yourself up for not having it, and, more than likely, you will have a complete manuscript.

Last example. You're going to lose x amount of weight by Christmas. Nope. How about your accountability partner will make sure you go to the gym at least three days a week, eat junk food only once a week, and limit your caloric intake to whatever your ideal is?

Again, if you follow the process, I bet you will achieve your goal, but there's no beating yourself up should you miss it. What will happen is you lose twenty pounds instead of twenty-five, and you're not crushing your self-esteem.

Sometimes, we forget to look back and see just how far we've come.

Wherever possible, stick to process goals and not outcome goals. According to mental coach Lanny Bassham, author of the brilliant book "With Winning in Mind," they're much healthier psychologically.

Alright, onto the next chapter, where you're going to learn why it's imperative that you write your goals down and not type them out or try and keep them in your head.

KEY POINTS

- Big goals can be daunting and cause people to give up before they start.
- Break goals into sub-goals.
- Reverse engineering is an easy way to figure out what steps to take.
- Not every goal can be reverse-engineered.
- If you fail to plan, you've planned to fail.
- If it's not an outcome goal, try to make it a process goal.

INSCRIBED

The I in A.S.P.I.R.E. stands for **"Inscribed."** You're going to want to write your goals down. Whether that's in a journal, a page you stick on the wall, or Post-It notes like the great Jeffrey Gitomer, the benefits of doing so have been proven many times. There's something about writing your goals on paper that gets them into your head better than just thinking about them.

The very act of writing involves visual, kinesthetic, and auditory senses. Visual because you're watching your words take shape on the page as you write them. Kinesthetic because you're holding your pen or pencil and you can feel the contact between pen and paper. (Have you ever had a specific pen and a particular type of paper that, when combined, feel amazing to write with?) Auditory because you're listening to your internal dialogue as you write.

Dr. Carol Quinn (Ph.D. at Syracuse University) talks about the efficacy of the teaching model, which involves writing, discussion, and reading, as a far more beneficial method of learning than just sitting in on a lecture.

In a study at the University of Indiana, scientists used a Magnetic Resonance Imaging machine (MRI) on children to monitor their brain activity while writing on paper. They discovered that writing engages massive areas of the brain, which are involved in thinking, memory, and language.

Add to the above the recent re-conceptualization of the connection between thinking and writing. Previously, writing on paper was merely meant to record what one thought. The new view is that writing develops thinking.

Something else to consider: if you don't write your goals down, how will you remember them? When I learned to fly, we had a checklist that we went through on whatever aircraft we would fly that day. Trusting that to memory could have been disastrous. Can you imagine someone trying to build a house without a plan or blueprints and trying to remember how it was all laid out in his head?

The Association for Psychological Science reported that students who physically took notes by writing on paper received a memory boost, especially compared to those who took notes on a laptop.

If you still need convincing, think of how often you've been shopping without a list and come back home only to discover you've forgotten something you needed. Everybody's done this. So, if you can't remember items you need ten minutes after leaving the house, how will you justify committing something as important as your goals, your blueprint for your life, to your memory?

"Fill your paper with the breathings of your heart." - William Wordsworth

In an impromptu study by Marc Levy in the book "Accidental Genius", Levy talks about surreptitiously making notes of students' plans while talking to them. Only moments later, Levy asked students to recount what they'd been talking about; on average, they remembered only half of what they'd told him.

Writing down your goals also allows you to revisit them often and ponder them at length. It lays them out logically and aids with the planning phase we mentioned previously, especially with setting sub-goals.

Journals Rule

As an interesting aside, you could write goals down on a cheap legal pad, but you really might want to consider buying a nice pen and an expensive, leather-bound journal to write them down. One simple idea could end up being worth millions of dollars.

Jim Rohn once commented that he would spend twenty-five dollars on a leather-bound journal because he was guaranteed to put at least twenty-five dollars' worth of good ideas in it.

Brain Health

Utilizing your brain does more than help with your goals. Robert S. Wilson, Ph.D. (neuropsychologist) said, "Exercising your brain, by writing, for example, from childhood through old age, is essential for brain health." In his study at the University Medical Center in Chicago, he found that the people who stimulated their brains had a slower rate of decline in memory than those who didn't. The study found that the rate of decline was reduced by thirty-two percent in people with frequent activities such as writing and reading.

Writing V Typing

Psychological scientists Pam A. Mueller of Princeton University and Daniel M. Oppenheimer of the University of California tested note-taking versus laptop writing. Across the board, the note-taking crew performed better. In three separate studies, those who took notes via a laptop performed worse on conceptual questions than students who took notes longhand. The laptop users tended to transcribe lectures verbatim, whereas the longhand writers processed the information and reframed it in their own words.

A study at Indiana University determined writing goals with a pen or pencil engaged more areas of the brain than using a keyboard. The reason is simple. To form a letter, you have to think about writing it. Does the stroke of the letter go up or down, where does the next stroke begin, and where does it end? That will change depending on the following letter. Compare that to simply touching a key on a keyboard, where you don't have to think about the letter formation at all.

Let's not forget Grant Cardone, the best-selling author of "10X Rule" and "If You're Not First, You're Last," a multi-millionaire who was broke at age twenty-five. He writes his top five goals twice a day. He does this first thing upon getting up in the morning and last thing before going to bed at night. He poses the question at his seminar: Who has a better chance of achieving his goals? The guy who writes them over 700 times in a year, or the guy who writes them down once on the first of January?

Alright. In the next chapter, you'll learn that the letter R stands for two elements and why they're essential.

KEY POINTS

- Writing something down is more effective than trusting it to memory.
- Writing engages more of the brain than texting or typing.
- Writing gives you a record that you can revisit.
- Writing gives you a product that you can share with your accountability partner.
- Writing gives you a memory boost.
- Writing frees up space in your head.
- Writing is important for your brain health.

REWARDED/RESOURCES

L ike the "S" in A.S.P.I.R.E., the "R" represents two subjects. The first is for **"Rewarded,"** and the second is for **"Resources."**

Rewards

Regarding rewards, two large-scale studies conducted on goal setting by noted U.K. scientist Richard Wiseman found that the most successful people rewarded their achievements for small sub-goals and larger primary goals.

We've been training people and pets that way for years. Reward the behavior you want to see more of and ignore what you want to see less of.

Intrinsic V Extrinsic

More recent research has delved into intrinsic and extrinsic rewards. For example, intrinsic rewards are internalized, such as a sense of accomplishment or a feeling of a job well done.

On the other hand, extrinsic rewards are monetary rewards, ribbons, trophies, and promotions. While such studies have gone into great depth about which is more effective, the simple answer is to figure out which works best for you and reward yourself accordingly.

Keep in mind the rewards do not have to be huge or expensive. It could be as simple as treating yourself to your favorite dessert after checking off one of the smaller steps on the way to a significant goal. It might be to buy a new pair of jeans or the song you want to add to your collection. Maybe it's a day off work to sit in the park and chill out for an afternoon.

The only thing you need to be careful of is that rewarding yourself with a chocolate bar doesn't make sense if you've just lost the first five pounds toward the primary goal of losing twenty pounds by Christmas.

Make it work in conjunction with whatever the goal is and not at odds with it. In the preceding example of losing weight, you might treat yourself to a massage at a local spa or buy the new shoes you've been eyeing for a while. Or, it could be buying the new dress/jeans in the smaller size you now fit into.

"Water the root to enjoy the fruit."
-Maharishi Mahesh Yogi

One important key is to reward yourself as soon as possible after completing your sub-goal. Studies show that linking the two events has much more impact when done close to each other rather than further apart. In other words, a coach who yells "well done" to someone scoring a goal will have more impact on that behavior than the coach telling the player after the game.

This might be one reason we're losing the fight against crime. Typically, criminals get arrested several days, weeks, or months after they commit the crime. Then, they're usually released back into society until their trial date. Next, they get several continuances in court while they plead and seek legal counsel. To add insult to injury, when they finally go to trial and are found guilty, oftentimes, the sentencing isn't done on the same day.

By punishing someone – eventually – for a crime they committed months or years earlier, we're not helping the miscreants make the connection, which is, arguably, part of the problem. Catching people red-handed has always been an incredibly effective method of deterring them from future anti-social behavior.

Incidentally, this is why punishing your dog when you come home and find trash on the floor is a complete waste of time. Despite how many pet owners insist to the contrary (by claiming the dog looks guilty), he cannot link the punishment and act of pulling out the trash. You must catch him in the act if you want the punishment to be effective.

I know some pet owners are reading this now, insisting I'm wrong and they're right. Mr. Fluffington absolutely knows that he's being punished for pulling out the trash. Why, he even looks guilty.

Do you want to bet? Here's a simple test to prove that Fido can't link the two if you're open-minded enough to follow through and do it.

Dog Psychiatrist

This study came from a friend of mine who's a shrink for dogs. I know. It sounds weird, but he decided to work with pets after being shot out one night while doing hostage negotiations at a SWAT standoff.

Bring your dog into the kitchen and let him watch while YOU dump the trash all over the floor. Now, go outside, wait about five minutes, and then enter the house. I guarantee your dog will be cowering in the kitchen, waiting for the punishment you usually administer because the trash is on the floor.

How can this be? If you're right about him looking guilty when HE pulls out the trash, he should be happy to see you and wagging his tail. That's because he knows he didn't pull it out. You did. He just watched you do it.

So why is he cowering? Because he's linked trash on the floor when you come home to being punished. He can't connect pulling the trash out and getting it on the floor later. He's a dog, not a person. Catch him in the act; yes, a correction is in order. Come home later and find evidence of an accident. Clean it up, leave the dog alone, and wait until you catch them in the act.

Carrot Or Stick?

Rewards on their own, by the way, are just as effective as rewards and punishment or carrot and stick. People learned this the first time they tried to train dolphins. If you try to punish a dolphin, he simply swims away, so you have to use rewards only. If you've ever been to an aquarium and watched them perform, you can see firsthand how effective that method is.

RESOURCES

When you're setting your goals, you're going to need to make two lists with regard to resources. The first is a list of resources you currently have. The second is a list of resources you're going to need.

Obviously, each goal will require different resources, so list the resources you both have and need for each goal.

You're going to want to consider the following when listing existing resources:

- Skills
- Knowledge,
- Networks,
- Time,
- Money or lines of credit,
- Emotional or Psychological strengths

It might also help you figure out how you can leverage each one of those to help you achieve your aims.

The next step is going to be to work out what resources you're going to need that you don't already have.

These might include things like

- Additional Skills
- Technology
- Specific tools you require
- A mentor

Then, you might want to prioritize the missing elements. It's entirely possible you need some immediately to get your project underway, whereas others can wait till later.

You might want to also factor in alternatives and plan Bs if you can't get hold of a particular resource or there's a scarcity. This might involve creative problem-solving, collaboration, or finding alternative resources.

Resource Management

Next, depending on your goal, don't forget about resource management. Money, for example, can be burned through at a prodigious rate if you're not careful. The old rule of thumb of "factor how much money you think you'll need and then double it, and add half again" has never proved wrong in my experience.

Included in that is devoting some time to thinking about sustainability. Should it take longer than you expected, do you have a plan to replenish resources over time?

FYI: Don't neglect psychological and emotional resources either. Many people don't factor either of these in to their detriment.

Your goals may require resilience, fortitude, and a growth mindset. You will run into inevitable setbacks as you strive for the finish line.

You may as well include your support system in those resources. Family, friends, mentors, and colleagues can all provide support and practical help. Don't forget your accountability partner is one of these resources because they are holding your feet to the fire to ensure you achieve your goals.

So, here's a quick example of what all the above might look like if you decided to write a book, for example.

Your existing resources might include a computer, a word processor, a printer, paper, and an idea.

Resources you might be missing could include software designed explicitly for authors, an agent, a content editor, a cover designer; particular knowledge on formatting the book so you can upload it to Amazon; knowledge of how to market the book; a website wizard to build your author's website; and a plan outlining how many words you need to write each day, etc.

Remember what I said about prioritizing your resources. In the above list, you can start with what you already have. You're not going to need the cover design, formatter, or editor until you've already done your first draft and your three or four (or more) rewrites.

Now, there's only the letter "E" to go. Like the "S" and "R," which both represent two different elements, the "E" in ASPIRE does the same.

KEY POINTS

- People given rewards were more successful at achieving goals.
- Rewards don't have to be big to be effective.
- The sooner you receive the reward after achieving one of the steps in the goal, the more effective they are.
- Don't make the reward counterproductive. (i.e., cake for losing weight).
- You have to divide resources into those you have and those you need
- Your resources should be prioritized. Remember, you probably won't need them all at once.
- Resources can include mental and emotional aspects
- Resources will have to be managed, and you will have to factor in alternatives sometimes.

EXCLUSIVE/EMOTIONAL

Finally, the E in A.S.P.I.R.E., like the S and the R, stands for two things. The first is **"Emotional"** and the second is **"Exclusive."** Concerning the latter, if the goal isn't yours exclusively, it's unlikely you'll achieve it, or if you do, you'll be unhappy that you did so.

Exclusivity

Think of how many people went to college and earned a degree because their parents wanted them to or because it was expected of them.

Hell, maybe you're one of them. Consider doctors who are doctors and dentists who are dentists only because their fathers and grandfathers were all doctors and dentists, respectively. A girlfriend of mine is begrudgingly working through her M.B.A. to appease her parents even though she is an entrepreneur at heart and wants to escape corporate America.

So many fellow Legionnaires had run away from their lives to escape such drudgery. One in particular that I did basic training with had been a dentist in civilian life in Belgium. He'd done it because his father and grandfather were both dentists, and it was expected of him. Finally, one day, he'd had enough, and he walked out the door and joined the Legion. He was as happy as a clam because he was finally doing something that had been one of his lifelong goals. He told me during basic training that he never told the interviewers at the intake center he'd been a dentist because he was afraid they might make him do the same thing in the Legion.

Here's another example of why exclusivity is essential. As a hypnotist certified in smoking cessation, I will occasionally run into a potential client who's in my office because his wife wants him to quit. I've also had people call who want me to help their parents stop.

They get a little bit miffed when they find out I can't make someone do something with hypnosis that they don't want to do. Unless that potential client wants to stop smoking for themselves, it will never happen. Once again, the goal must be yours.

Emotional

Secondly, if the goal is emotional, you will stick with it during the inevitable hurdles and roadblocks that life will throw in front of you while you pursue it. If it's something that someone else wants you to do or something you think would be nice to do and relatively easy, then it won't survive first contact with any obstacles. Also, staying motivated with a goal such as "having a retirement home in the South of France overlooking the ocean" is more straightforward than setting one like "having enough for retirement."

Another word instead of emotional (in case that sounds a bit strong) is "reason." What is your reason for wanting this particular goal? If you can't answer that, it's probably not compelling enough to see it through to its conclusion.

In the Legion, we had a group called CRAPs[2] which was an acronym that stood for "Commandos de Recherché et d'Action dans la Profondeur." In English, they were a group of Commandos who specialized in deep penetration information gathering and a pathfinder unit. These guys were the crème de la crème of the Legion and the French military.

To begin with, you had to be a volunteer upon leaving basic training with the Legion to make it into the parachute unit. Once there, you had to make the rank of Corporal and then apply to do the grueling selection test. Part of it included a half marathon

---

[2] CRAP is now called Groupment Commando Parachutists. I have no idea if this was due to any connotation of the English meaning of their acronym or not.

through the mountains of Corsica in full combat gear, followed immediately by a half-kilometer swim.

In conclusion, you had to swim fifty meters underwater without surfacing for a breath. Once the pool session was over, you ran to the gym to climb ropes and do push-ups and sit-ups, all within a specific time frame.

Come in one second over; you're not welcome in the group. Once you make it into the unit (which is small), training begins in earnest, and these guys get to go on every single course the French military offers. It's an impressive list, including sniper training, demolitions, skydiving on oxygen, hand-to-hand combat, shipboard diving, river crossing diver, commando, mountain climbing, medical, etc.

Within our group was a Corporal named Tossalini, who desperately wanted to be a specialist unit member but had been denied twice for being deemed too old. Talk about being emotional about a particular goal; the next time the company went up to jump, he unhooked the static line on his parachute and went out the door at 800 meters on his reserve chute. Unlike his main, which opened automatically, the reserve required opening by pulling the ripcord manually.

He figured if he went out, he'd prove to the powers that be that he had the necessary qualities to be a unit member. It was a pretty bold move. If his reserve had failed him, there was no backup, and while the GCP do indeed free-fall, they typically do it between 13,000 and 18,000 feet, giving them plenty of time to sort stuff out if it goes wrong. At 800 meters, Tossalini had about four seconds to open his eyes before he would have made a big hole in the ground.

Unfortunately for him, he didn't get accepted and ended up in the brig for a few days, but it's a fine example of how one will cross any obstacle if they feel strongly enough about their goal.

Some of you have no doubt heard of the example where a father had tried many times to quit smoking and hadn't been able to last more than a few weeks before smoking again. He felt compelled to see it through when his young daughter walked in one day crying her eyes out. She had watched a graphic anti-smoking film at school and didn't think he would live long enough to be able to give her away when she got married. That was the day he quit. Emotions are potent.

KEY POINTS

- Goals should be yours and yours alone.
- If your heart isn't in it, the chances of success dwindle.
- Emotion is a massive driving force.
- Knowing your "why" is all-important.

GOALS

Before we begin this section, let's talk about the elephant in the room. Many gurus, corporate trainers, and coaches regurgitate this story about the famous Harvard or Yale goal studies. I'm talking about some of the biggest names in the personal development industry.

No Yale or Harvard Goal Study

Depending on which guru you listen to, the Yale study was allegedly conducted in 1953, while the Harvard version comes from 1979. Both of them have remarkably similar findings. Allegedly, 3% of students who'd written their goals down had amassed more money than the other 97% combined when they followed up with them twenty years later.

The only problem is that neither study ever took place. They were both researched by Lawrence Tabak of Fast Company, and there's no evidence that either existed.

Now, that doesn't mean that setting goals isn't necessary. On the contrary, we've discovered that every company sets them, and they bind every project. We landed on the moon because President Kennedy set a goal to do so. It's the way corporations inspire their workers and can map their progress.

Regarding science and ignoring the fabricated "Yale & Harvard Studies," a 2015 study at Dominican University showed that when people wrote their goals down, they were 42% more successful than those who didn't (Matthews, 2015).

Further research (Kleingeld, Van Mierlo, Arends, 2011) uncovered aspects of goal setting and its link to being successful. Finally, goal setting has been linked to self-confidence, motivation, and autonomy (Locke & Latham, 2006).

Unclear Goals

In the military, almost everything starts and ends with a goal or clear-cut objective in mind (or at least it should). And, just like in the military, whatever your particular mission is, i.e., to get a raise, buy a vacation home, buy a Ferrari, spend more time with the kids, make a million dollars, travel around the world, etc., it should begin with a clearly defined plan on exactly how you intend to achieve that particular objective. If it doesn't, you're not giving yourself the best possible chance of achieving it.

"You can have anything you want. You just can't have everything you want."
- Ben Rouse.

I never cease to be amazed at how many people I meet who don't have clearly defined goals. I heard the famous American business philosopher Jim Rohn talk about the time he met his mentor, Earl Shoef. Shoef asked Rohn for his list of goals, and when Rohn couldn't produce a list, Shoef told him, "Then I can tell you, within a couple of hundred dollars, how much money you have in your bank account." As Rohn went on to explain, Shoef was absolutely right.

"People who regularly write down their goals earn nine times as much over their lifetimes as the people who don't, and yet 80% of Americans say they don't have goals. Sixteen percent do have goals, but they don't write them down. Less than four percent write their goals down, and fewer than one percent review them on an ongoing basis."
- Professor Emeritus Dave Kohl.

Like any successful organization, the powers that be in the Legion do not wake up every morning and ask themselves, "So, what are we going to do today?" They have plans for that day, that week, that month, that year, and that decade.

The same is true of any corporation, company, or organization considered credible by the public and their shareholders. Can you imagine the board at General Motors walking in every morning and having a meeting on what they should work on that day? Those guys already have plans for their company's direction and know which vehicles they will release over the next ten years.

For example, a quick Google search showed the following by Starbucks.

Starbucks chief executive officer Kevin Johnson announced Tuesday a renewed focus on sustainability, all with an eye toward eventually *"giving more than we take from the planet."*

"Our aspiration is to become resource positive -- storing more carbon than we emit, eliminating waste, and providing more clean freshwater than we use," Johnson wrote in a letter posted Tuesday.

His letter included preliminary targets for 2030 and the company's commitment to be transparent in its reporting against short- and long-term goals. He also vowed to work with Starbucks partners, customers, and other stakeholders on this journey. He wrote that the company will spend the next year continuing to test and learn before formalizing these sustainability targets as part of the company's 50th anniversary in 2021.

"Our eyes are wide open knowing that we do not have all the answers or fully understand all the complexities and potential consequences," Johnson wrote. *"Now, it's time to create an even broader aspiration – and it's work that will require visionary thinking, new ways of working, investment of resource, and urgent action."*

Here are five important things to know about Tuesday's announcement:

1. Starbucks wants to halve its carbon emissions, waste output, and water impact in the next decade while growing the business at the same time

> Johnson's letter outlined three preliminary targets: By 2030, Starbucks will aim to reduce carbon emissions by 50 percent; reduce waste sent to landfills from stores and manufacturing by 50 percent, driven by a broader shift toward a circular economy; and will also conserve or replenish 50 percent of the water currently being used for direct operations and coffee production.

There's more to the quote, but did you notice that his letter stretched all the way out to 2030? I found similar examples for Disney, Pepsi, and Lowes.

If this long-term planning is working for these guys, why do you think you can pull off your idea of success on a day-to-day basis? The simple answer is you can't, yet this is precisely what most people try and do, which is probably why most people aren't successful.

You absolutely have to steal a page from the Fortune 500's playbook and set your goals. There is no other way. Of course, making a list of them isn't enough. You must also learn how to set them out logically and use a scientifically validated method to ensure you achieve them. That's precisely what we will do in this section. Remember, we're less interested in goal setting than we are in goal achievement.

"A goal properly set is halfway to being achieved."

-   Zig Ziglar

First Exposure

My first exposure to goal setting was when my older brother, Tony (RIP), attended a seminar by the American business philosopher Jim Rohn.

It was Rohn's first-ever seminar in Australia, and four years later, my brother had a net worth that put him in the millionaire category (and this was back in the late seventies and early eighties when a million still meant something). He was a bricklayer (or mason as they're known in the United States) running a one-man show fixing up barbeques and fences.

In the four years following the seminar, he attained his master builder's license, hired a crew, formed a company, and began building houses and shopping centers. His company, Down Under, was one of the first to come up with the idea of bricking in underneath Australian homes. Many of them are built on stumps, and his company would turn that previously wasted space into something useful. The clearly defined goals my brother learned about at the seminar paved the way for his ultimate success.

After talking to my brother about the process he'd learned in the seminar, I realized that it was remarkably similar to the process I'd learned during my lifelong study of the martial arts.

Black Belt Goal Setting

The colored belt system of Judo – the first art I ever studied – is a perfect example of goal setting. You begin as a neophyte and signify this by wearing a white belt to demonstrate purity and innocence. You start to learn a set of basic techniques that you must master and demonstrate proficiency in, and once you've done this, you take a test to prove that you have perfected them.

Assuming you pass the test, you learn some progressively more intricate and complicated techniques, at which point you will test again. You continue doing this from a white belt through yellow, orange, green, blue, brown, and finally, the coveted black belt. In other words, there are clearly defined goals, and you progress when you hit them.

We live in a world that screams "GO, GO, GO"

without telling us

"WHERE, WHERE, WHERE."

Nick Hughes

My brother's path was no different. He needed a set of skills to achieve his company's ultimate goal, which was to secure his financial future and make him rich in the process. He had to learn how to oversee an entire job site, study for and pass his master builder's permit, learn about marketing, advertising, bookwork, hiring and firing, public relations, and so on until he could put it all together and make it happen.

One could just as easily apply a colored belt ranking system to what he did, culminating in his "black belt" when he launched Down Under. Indeed, hasn't Six Sigma done precisely that by applying martial arts belt grades to denote the skill levels of their practitioners?

In the military, it is precisely the same format. We're given a mission to accomplish and, whether it's rescuing hostages in Zaire, helping the allies in Desert Shield/Storm, escorting gold bullion to French troops in Mexico, rescuing kidnapped French school children in Somalia, protecting the Aerospatiale Missile Launching site in Guyana, South America or protecting the Nuclear Testing Facility on Muroroa Atoll, it's done in the same fashion. We calculate the desired result, determine what skills and equipment are needed to make that happen, plan it all out to the nth degree, and execute.

Can you see the common denominator here? It doesn't matter if it's school, college, university, martial arts, the military, or corporate America; every single, successful entity uses goal setting to set their sights, make their plans, and go for them.

We live in a society and a day and age that screams "Go, Go, Go" without telling us "Where, Where, Where." Goals give us the "where, where, where" by becoming waypoints on a map with a starting point and a clearly defined destination.

KEY POINTS

- Every successful organization in the world has goals.
- Goals give us a target, and a target give us weapons.
- I've never worked for a multi-millionaire who didn't have them.
- People who write them down make nine times as much as people who don't.
- The "famous" Harvard & Yale studies do not exist.

THE GOALS WORKSHOP

GOALS PART II

Alright. So, how do you actually choose goals now that you know you should choose ones that matter to you? What follows is an exercise very similar to what we used to do in the Legion to come up with the best way to tackle an objective: brainstorming. Everyone sat around and started tossing out ideas with the understanding no idea would be shouted down or thought stupid or trivial. If you do the latter, people clam up and only offer ideas they think are good.

You want to be like the professional photographer who takes thousands of pictures to get one or two that work. As the ideas flowed, they created other ideas in people's minds, who would then offer those. Once we had our pile of ideas, then, and only then, did we sift through them to find out which ones might be the most effective. We also applied tests to them to see if they stood up to scrutiny, but before we did that, we created our monster list of ideas first.

Step One: You must do the same thing with your goals. Take out a legal pad or a bunch of paper and start by writing down.

- all the things you want to have,
- all the things you want to do,
- all the things you want to be,
- all the places you want to visit, etc.

Don't let reality get in the way here. Just like sitting on an idea that you think is dumb during the brainstorming session, not writing something down because you think it will never happen might deprive you of achieving something that you really want.

Play a game and suspend disbelief. Pretend for a moment that you CAN have it all. If this idea bothers you, remember what Bruce Lee said, "A goal is not always meant to be reached. It often serves simply as something to aim at," or what W. Clement Stone said, "Aim for the moon, if you miss, you may hit a star."

The funny thing is, many people struggle with this — especially when you're alone and not sitting around with a group of fellow Legionnaires piggybacking off their ideas. What will help is doing the exercise with complete abandon. In other words, don't apply any self-imposed limitations for this portion of the workshop.

If nothing was in your way, if money wasn't an object, if age didn't matter, if physical size, shape, and attributes were not an issue, answer the above questions. The idea is to return to that child-like state with no limitations. Playing music while you do this will often help if you're struggling. I'm not sure why that is, but I've seen it work too many times to dismiss the idea out of hand.

Child Like State

If you're unsure what that child-like state means, let me tell you about something I observed visiting my friend Ernie years ago. At the time, Ernie was a schoolteacher, and I visited him in his classroom in New Jersey. He told his students I was an artist, and the conversation concerned art and drawing.

When he asked those kids, "How many of YOU can draw?" every kid in that classroom put their hands up. Now, anytime you ask that question of a room full of adults, only a handful put their hands up. Why is that? What happens to those kids who are convinced they have no artistic ability by the time they're adults? I'd bet too many people telling them they couldn't draw destroyed their creative spark.

I witnessed this one firsthand. My ex had painted when she was younger and quit after an art teacher told her she had no talent. I kept on and on at her that she needed to get back into it after seeing some of her work, and finally, one day, she busted out the paints and painted a stunning canvas. It is the perfect blend of colors and balanced composition with no formal training. So much for the art teacher. He was probably the same type of teacher who told Thomas Edison that he was too stupid to learn anything, and I'd be willing to bet her critic probably never sold any paintings either.

So, tap into your inner child and go wild. Write, and don't stop writing till you've compiled a list of all the above things, no matter how crazy they might seem. Given such loose parameters, it shouldn't be too hard to compile a list of at least 200 goals.

127 Things

If you want an idea of what to look for, check out John Goddard's website (www.JohnGoddard.info). Goddard is famous for writing a list of 127 things he wanted to do before he died. He wrote his list when he was only fifteen years old. He passed away in 2013 and completed 109 of them, and when you go check out his website, you'll realize how impressive that is.

Another person to check out is Nik Halik, author of the "5 Day Weekend" and labeled a trillionaire in his home country of Australia. He wrote down ten goals when he was eight and achieved all but two of them at the time of writing. So you're appropriately impressed, here's his list:

1. To walk on the moon.
2. To go to the space station and live there.
3. To become an astronaut.
4. To own beautiful places all over the world.
5. To travel and explore more than 100 countries.
6. Go to the bottom of the ocean and have lunch on the deck of the Titanic.
7. To become a mountain climber and climb the highest mountains in the world.
8. To run with the bulls in Spain.
9. To become a millionaire.
10. To become a rock & roll star.

The only two he hasn't accomplished (yet) are walking on the moon and living in the space station. I bet he'll do both before he casts off his mortal coil.

What Don't You Want?

Another trick to try if you're struggling, which taps into man's propensity for going after the negative, is to try and write down all the things you DON'T want. That can sometimes help you come up with what you seek.

In other words, I don't want to become bankrupt. That might give you a goal to build a financial fortress around yourself, get a financial planner, or marry an accountant.

I don't want to end up in the hospital having had a heart attack might lead you to establish a goal to become healthy.

I don't want to be one of those parents who never have time for their kids, might create the goal of spending more time with them.

Here are some other ideas to get the ball rolling.

Personal Goals

- Would you like to speak another language? If yes, which one(s)?
- What countries would you like to visit?
- What landmarks in your own country haven't you seen?
- Would you like to learn how to dance?
- Learn how to cook?
- Take acting lessons?
- Act in a play or a movie?
- Move to a different part of town?

- Learn how to SCUBA dive?
- Swim with the dolphins?
- Volunteer?
- What character traits would you like to develop?
- What skills would you like to learn?
- Learn how to hypnotize people.
- Learn to touch type?
- Re-connect with old friends?
- Forgive?
- Join Toastmasters?
- Paint the house?
- Attend a film premiere?
- Get invited to the White House?
- Would you like a maid?
- Do you want a personal chef?
- How about a butler or a chauffeur?
- Teach someone how to read?
- Join a charity group or organization?
- Get a coach?
- Do stand-up comedy

Career Goals

- How much do you want to earn?
- How far up in the company do you want to go?

- Do you want to own your own business? If yes, doing what?
- Would you like to take your existing business public?
- Do you want to change careers and do something more challenging?
- Do you want an MBA?
- Do you want a mentor?
- Do you want to become a mentor?
- Do you want to write a book about the business you're in?
- Do you want to expand into other markets?
- When do you want to retire?
- Where do you want to retire to?
- What plans do you have for retirement?
- Do you want to work for SCORE?
- Run for local office?
- Mentor someone at work?

Health & Fitness Goals

- Do you want to be in great shape?
- How about having a six-pack?
- Do you want to quit smoking?
- Do you have an ideal weight?

- Do you want a personal trainer?
- Cut back on drinking?
- Do cardio a certain amount of times per week?
- Join a gym?
- Buy a push bike?
- Learn to Rollerblade?
- Learn to windsurf?
- Start running – a marathon, spartan race, triathlon, etc.?
- Lower your blood pressure?
- Lower your cholesterol?
- Get a checkup?
- Learn yoga?
- Learn a martial art?
- Have an operation to repair a niggling injury?

Financial Goals

- Do you want to max out your 401k?
- Do you want to start investing twenty percent of what you make?
- Thirty percent?
- Forty percent?
- How much do you want to make this year?

- How much do you want to be making five years from now?
- How much do you want to be making ten years from now?
- Are you debt-free?
- When do you want to retire?
- How much do you want saved/invested to retire on?
- How about being financially independent?
- What's your net worth going to be?
- Do you want to put kids through college?
- What are you going to invest in?
- How much is your dream house worth?
- Do you want a financial fortress that nobody can get through around you and your family?
- Would you always like to walk around with five hundred cash on you? How about $1,000?
- Would you like a black American Express Card?

Toys for Boys and Girls Goals

- What sort of car do you want? A Porsche, a Ferrari? A Lamborghini?
- What brand of watch?
- Do you want a vacation home?

- Own a plane or private jet?

- Where do you want to go on vacation?

- Take a round-the-world trip?

- Do you want a mansion?

- Own a motorbike?

- Do you want a yacht?

- Do you want a maid?

- Do you want a cook?

- How about a butler?

- What about a chauffeur?

- How about a Maybach for him to drive you around in?

- A personal assistant?

- A private island like Sir Richard Branson?

- An art collection?

Family Goals

- Do you want to spend more quality time with the kids?

- Do you want to get married?

- Do you want to get divorced?

- Do you want to forgive someone?

- Do you want to take the family on a vacation?

- Pay for your kid's college?

- Buy your kid a car?

- Get a dog/cat?

- Move to a bigger house?

- Pay for your daughter's wedding?

- Get braces for the children?

- Put in a pool?

- Buy a hot tub?

Accomplishment Goals

- Provide for your family?

- Have life insurance in the event something happens?

- Write a book?

- See the world?

- Have no regrets about what you didn't do?

- Leave a legacy?

- Give back to the community in which you live?

- Give back to the world?

- Raise productive children?

- Raise healthy children?

- Make peace with your enemies?

- Make peace with yourself?

- Help build a Habitat for Humanity home?

- Teach someone to read or write?

- Leave the world a better place than you found it?

- Adopt a child?
- Visit children in hospital?
- Volunteer with the Red Cross?
- Join Big Brother/Big Sister?

Unbelievable

Another tip for you. Think about the categories above and then devise a goal for each that makes you say "Unbelievable." That's the reaction I've had a few times as a bodyguard when I've seen where some of my clients live and what they fly and drive. One had a watch worth over 100,000 pounds that I had to take to the store for a cleaning. Another had a two-story penthouse in Boca Raton, Florida, overlooking the beach. I've seen private jets and Maybachs in my travels, private islands, private runways, and mega yachts.

What would make you say "Wow" or "Unbelievable" in each category? Remember, at this point, it doesn't matter if you think you can ever achieve any of that or not. Get it down as part of the exercise. Nothing is off limits, and nothing is too grandiose.

Step Two: Alright, now that you've compiled your list, go back through them and separate them into

- short-term goals (those that take a year or less),

- medium-term goals (those that take between one and three years to complete), and finally,
- long-term goals (those that take longer than three years to achieve).

You might notice a pattern here. Some people discover they have many short-term goals and very few or no long-term goals. Others find the opposite, i.e., they have many long-range goals but no short-term ones.

There's no wrong or right in this; it is merely an interesting observation that may make you reconsider whether your planning is too long or short-range in scope.

Personally, I don't make any further than ten years out because I believe, based on empirical evidence in my own life, that too much can happen, and making plans that are far away isn't prudent or necessary. There hasn't been a single time when I've been sitting somewhere thinking, *"If someone told me I'd be doing this ten years ago, I'd have told them they were crazy."*

That's true of being a black belt, being in the Legion, flying in private jets, and lying on the roof of a tattoo studio in North Carolina watching a lunar eclipse with a woman. I'm sure that, ten years from now, that will be true again. Everyone is different, though. If you want to go out for as long as twenty years and create your perfect life, feel free to do so.

Step Three: Now you've got to sort the twelve-month goals out until you narrow it down to no less than four and no more than ten of them that you intend to complete this year. These goals, or objectives, should be challenging.

Harder Is Better

The latest scientific research has proven that challenging and somewhat tricky goals are far more likely to be accomplished than easy goals. I could spend five pages writing why that is and how the brain works, but that's not the book's purpose.

As Jim Rohn used to say, *"Some people study the roots while others are out picking the fruit."* If it's too easy, you won't rise to the challenge, it won't be worth putting your money or reputation on the line, and it will probably be more of a task than a goal.

BHAGs

Some say you need at least one BHAG (pronounced Bee Hag) in each category. What's a BHAG? A Big, Hairy Audacious Goal. Think about the one the President gave NASA when he said, *"We are going to put a man on the Moon."* Now that's a BHAG.

Step Four. Now that you've picked out your list of objectives, we need to enter them into a format that makes them easy to work through. You can draw up a piece of paper or go to www.NickHughesCoaching.com and download a copy there. It doesn't matter how you get them down as long as you do.

You might want to make up your own three-leaf binder and put in a master list with some tabbed sections for each goal or break them down into short, medium, and long-term. Perhaps you'd rather keep them online or on your smartphone as a memo. Another option is to buy a journal and put it in there or buy the goal pages from people like Franklin Covey and use them in your planner.

The brilliant Jeffrey Gitomer, one of, if not the premier sales trainers in the United States, has a unique idea he calls his $100,000 idea, and he simply puts them on sticky notes on the left-hand side of his bathroom mirror. As he completes each goal, he moves it to the right-hand side of his mirror so he can

a) keep track of his unfinished goals and

b) have a constant reminder of his current set of goals.

He was kind enough to give me some of these, and it's one of the methods I use to keep mine where I see them daily.

Whichever system you opt to use on the pages devoted to each goal, you will notice, or need, a place to enter the goal and the date you entered it and then fill it out in the following order.

First: Pick one to two goals from each section of your master goal list. Make sure the ones you choose are indeed emotional and exclusive.

Second: Write down your goal and be specific. Go into as much detail as possible.

Third: Write down the planning phase. Break it into smaller pieces, and don't forget, if reverse engineering works here, use it.

Fourth: You want to make a list of resources. This list should include the ones you already have and those you will need.

Fifth: Make a list of the rewards you're going to enjoy as you check off each step.

Sixth: Get your accountability partner and figure out who you're pledging the money to, whether you're using two amounts or one, and who it's going to that will ensure you follow through.

Seventh: Share it on social media and with everyone you know.

In a little more detail, then. We start with emotional and exclusive before we decide on choosing our goal. (Yes, we covered this earlier in the book, but this will save you from having to flick back and forth between this section and the relevant chapters)

EMOTIONAL & EXCLUSIVE: This is the section where you choose your goals, ensuring that they are your goals and the ones you really desire. I usually do this with a highlighter, but you could also write them on a scrap piece of paper. Don't forget to take into account **why** you want it.

The why is hugely important. If the why (or reason) is big enough, the how will be figured out. In other words, where there's a will, there's a way—the how is also critical when writing down your goal steps or sub-goals. Your brain is wired to respond to how questions. If you write down, "I want a ten percent raise at work," as one of your goals, it will never be as effective as asking yourself, "How can I get a ten percent raise at work?" If you ask how, the incredibly powerful subconscious will go to work and figure out the way.

I'll never forget Dr. David Schwarz's section in "The Magic of Thinking Big" when he asked a group of college kids how they could possibly do away with prisons in five years. He wrote how they immediately started attacking the idea as crazy, telling him he was mad and could never be done.

He let them go on for a while and then pointed out, "How can we possibly do away with prisons?" and not, "What do you think of the idea of doing away with prisons." Once they understood that difference, their brains began to work on the "how," and the ideas started to flow thick and fast. They came up with youth programs, intervention plans, training in schools on crime prevention, social programs, and more.

Also, don't forget the other part of the letter "E" in A.S.P.I.R.E. is "exclusive." Double-check your goals and objectives and make sure they're one hundred percent yours. If you don't "own" them, you'll be tempted to give in when the going gets tough or miserable, even though you've achieved a goal. Remember what I wrote about hypnosis clients wanting to quit smoking?

Now that you have your rough list, we write them down.

INSCRIBED: Of course you're writing all this down, yes? Now, do you see the benefit of writing something instead of trying to keep it all in your head? The act of writing has made it tangible and given you something you can refer to on a daily basis.

And as we know from all of the studies, this writing process will engage more areas of the brain, improve critical thinking, help with recall, and more.

Another significant advantage of having goals written down is not just giving copies to your AP and sharing them on social media but also with a Mastermind group.

The concept comes from the book "Think & Grow Rich" by Napoleon Hill. Grab a few like-minded friends and arrange to meet once a month to review your goals with each other. This mastermind concept is massively powerful, and many of the ultra-rich I bodyguarded would meet like this regularly.

Next is what we write.

SPECIFICITY: Never forget that the goal must be specific if it will work. The more detail, the better. Which of the following is more compelling?

A: I will retire someday soon with a lot of money.

B: I will retire with a net worth of $2.5M by the 3rd of March, 2031. That money will come from a combination of living on 70 percent of what I earn, investing the 30 percent remaining, and leveraged income that I receive from a combination of developing online courses and buying rental properties.

I will read at least four books a year on personal finance, financial literacy, and investing. I will also look into attending financial seminars and listening to podcasts about wealth and managing my money.

Don't forget to go into this level of detail with every goal you set. The devil is in the details.

Now that you have your goal written down in detail, the next step is the planning phase.

PLANNING: Breaking your goal into manageable steps.

One of the easiest ways to do this is to reverse engineer your goal. For example, let's say your goal is to lose thirty pounds by the end of the year, and it is now January 1st. How much would you have needed to have lost by December 1st to be on track? Let's say twenty-eight pounds, for argument's sake.

That would make twenty-six pounds by November 1st,

twenty-four pounds by October 1st,

twenty-two by September 1st,

twenty by August 1st,

seventeen by July 1st,

fourteen by June 1st,

eleven pounds by May, 1st

eight by April 1st,

five pounds by March 1st,

three by February 1st,

and only two pounds to lose during January.

There's your example of setting baby steps and sub-goals.

If it's a goal that isn't so easy to quantify, i.e., something like launching your own business, you can still break them down into smaller sub-goals for our purposes.

Step one might be brainstorming and figuring out what type of business you want to be involved with.

Step two could be to look into all the available franchise opportunities.

Step three might be to interview business owners in that industry.

Step four could be subscribing to several applicable industry trade magazines.

Step five might be to join some online forums or user groups comprised of people in that industry.

Step six might be to rough out a business plan.

Step seven could be to meet with someone from SCORE[3].

Step eight might be meeting with potential investors or venture capitalists (depending on how much money you're looking at and how big the business you plan to launch).

---

[3] SCORE is an organization made up of retired executives from a plethora of industries. You can sit down with them and discuss your ideas about the business opportunity you're interested in and they'll be able to give you the benefit of their first-hand knowledge.

Step nine could be to meet with a commercial real estate broker, consider properties suitable for your purposes, and find out what they'll cost.

Step ten might be to break down the setting up of your new business into another set of sub-goals, for example, up-fitting the new location, hiring staff, purchasing office equipment, advertising and marketing, training the new hires, meeting with an attorney to incorporate, meeting the accountants to set up how you intend to structure the business, a brainstorming session with your IT guy and web designer, and so on.

You get the idea. No matter the goal, you need to break it down into smaller steps, which will a) make it more manageable and b) make it easier to measure your progress and verify whether you're on track.

These steps will also help you if you follow my earlier advice of thinking more about the process of the goals rather than the goal itself. In other words, rather than "lose thirty pounds," my process might be (revealed by the planning aspect of A.S.P.I.R.E.)

- restrict calories to 1900 six days a week,
- eliminate all sugars
- workout at least four days per week for thirty minutes a day
- eat OMAD (One meal a day) twice a week.

Remember that following the process and using your AP to ensure you stick to it can be better for your self-image/self-esteem than going for the goal itself. If you religiously follow the process, you'll probably hit your target, but you won't feel like a loser if you don't.

We do take things a couple of steps further in the military. After establishing our objective, we worked on the strategies needed. Then we act but constantly review and monitor how every operational phase is going and get prepared to be flexible and improvise when necessary.

Being too rigid in your planning is a sure way to fail, especially in the military when situations are fluid and dynamic and can change in a split second.

Before we push on to the rest of the breakdown of the goals, I'll give you an example of flexibility in play from my days as a bodyguard to the ultra-rich.

After finishing my time in the Legion, I was working on a close personal protection detail in London. Our team I was on had been tasked with looking after one of the Saudi princes, his wife, and his children during their stay in the city.

On this particular day, they were due to head to the airport on their private jet and return to the Middle East. The team leader told us they would leave the hotel soon and wanted me and another team member to accompany him and the family downstairs to the limousine.

The arrangement was that we'd escort the family to the car, at which point the team leader and only the team leader would travel with them in the limo to the airport. A backup team would follow in a chase vehicle.

Once they'd left, we would sweep the hotel rooms occupied by us and the family and terminate the gig until a meeting in the office the next day for a debrief.

Upon arrival downstairs, just as we'd put the family in the car, the Prince asked the team leader who else was traveling with them to the airport. He assumed two security personnel, not just the team leader, would be in the vehicle.

The team leader didn't even flinch. He just turned to look at us, and my colleague said, "That would be me." He moved to the passenger side front seat. (He lived near Heathrow airport, so it was easier for him to get home from there after the Prince and his family left than it would have been for me.)

It doesn't sound like much, but it was so fluid and fast that nobody watching would have been able to tell my colleague wasn't part of the plan from the outset. I went upstairs, joined the rest of the team for the sweeps, informed them what had happened, and packed my mate's bag so it could be returned to him later.

It could just as quickly have been a complete fiasco. We could have told the Prince, "Nobody told us we were coming...our bags are upstairs; you'll have to wait while we flip a coin and work out who's going, and they get their gear from upstairs." The point of my story is that flexibility is vital. You must be prepared during your planning phase to have that same flexibility in abundance.

Look at it this way: Plans can unravel due to unforeseen circumstances, and you must be ready. Don't let it daunt you. Nothing would ever get done if you weren't going to do anything unless conditions were perfect.

Don't believe me? Imagine you're going to travel to Disneyland with the kids from central Pennsylvania, but you aren't going to do so until conditions are perfect. That would mean there would be a guarantee of no accidents, no flat tires, no road work or detours, nobody getting sick, nobody forgetting something they'd left behind, perfect weather for the duration, no mechanical failures, and green lights all the way. When would you go on such a fantastic voyage? Exactly. Never. Instead, you plan your trip and be ready to be flexible en route.

Are there road works? Detour around them. Do you get a flat tire? Change it. Is there an accident? Providing nobody's hurt, exchange insurance information, and continue on your way. Is the weather bad? Turn on the wipers, slow down, exercise caution until conditions improve, and so on. It's not rocket science.

Remember the famous quote by Field Marshal Helmut von Moltke: "No plan survives first contact with the enemy" (summarized) or, as Mike Tyson said, "Everyone's got a plan till they get punched in the mouth."

As part of planning, you will want to make a list of all your resources. Remember, this will include the ones you have and a separate list of the ones you will need.

RESOURCES: Remember that there are two lists to make. The first is the resources you already have.

Those will include things like skills, knowledge, your network of friends and family, your time, your war chest, and your emotional and physical strengths.

The second list, the ones you might need, could include elements from the first list. In other words, you already have friends but may need to involve some more. The same may well occur with your money.

Consider resources like additional skills, technology, specific tools, a mentor, or a coach. Also, factor in resource management on this list. What if the money starts to run out? What if there's an argument with someone else involved?

Now, you'll want to make a quick list of the rewards you're going to enjoy as you complete each step.

REWARDED: Remember, as an organism, we tend to repeat behavior that we're rewarded for and stop doing that for which we get punished.

The only caveat is not to make the rewards counter-productive to your overall goal. In other words, if your goal is to lose thirty pounds, as in our previous example, it wouldn't behoove you to reward yourself with a massive chocolate sundae at the moment you lost your first two pounds.

If your goal was to save a certain amount of money to buy something, your reward shouldn't require spending money. Don't forget that the research shows it doesn't have to be a big reward to be effective. It can be something straightforward like a piece of your favorite candy, taking a few hours off to read a book, or seeing a movie.

Also, keep in mind the aforementioned intrinsic and extrinsic rewards system. Intrinsic rewards are internal rewards and not material. Extrinsic tends to be a material reward of some sort.

Some people respond more to a pat on the back and a well done (intrinsic) than to a cup, trophy, medal, or money (extrinsic). Figure out which one you are and write down your rewards accordingly.

At this point, you've chosen a select few goals from your master list, making sure they're exclusively yours and have a big enough why to motivate you.

You then wrote them out in detail, broke them down into smaller sub-tasks, and figured out how you would reward yourself when you completed each step.

Remember, this is where most goal-setting systems stop which is why they're okay for setting goals but not achieving them. Now is when you reach out to our accountability partner or coach and allocate the money and organization the money is going to should you not see the goal through.

ACCOUNTABILITY: Remember, that's the missing key to almost every self-help book in the market, so DO NOT skimp on this step if you're serious about achieving your goal. Write your check to someone or some organization you unequivocally hate/detest and give it to whoever your accountability partner is.

Remember, it MUST be someone who will follow through if you don't stick to your intended goal. It can't be your wife, brother, or best mate who, while full of good intentions when you start, will buckle down and tear up the checks when you start blubbering, pleading, crying, and whining about why you can't possibly stick to the goal and why you desperately need the money back, etc.

It also shouldn't be someone who, when they go ahead and cash your check, will be bothered if you never talk to them again if that's one of the lame threats you use to try and get them to cave in when crunch time comes. It must be a staunch person who will not cave under pressure.

I go as far as to have a legally binding contract drawn up that absolves the AP of any blame should they cash the checks if you don't stick to your goal. Another idea would be to use an attorney. He can place the money in an escrow account, and if you can't prove to him that you have accomplished the goal by a specific date, he can go ahead and send the check to the intended recipient.

Remember, I can't stress enough about this step. Use the AP for the goals that have to get done and that you're dead serious about. If you're not ready to be held accountable, then you're not serious about the goal, are you? If you don't want to be held responsible, return to that S.M.A.R.T. goal garbage and con yourself again.

Yet another option is to use a coach. If you don't have one of these and are in business, you're missing out on maximizing your potential. Every world-class athlete on the planet has a coach, from Tiger Woods to LeBron James and Michael Jordan to Usain Bolt. Yes, they're the best at what they do, but they still hire someone to ensure they do the work and put in the hours when they're not motivated. If you are an entrepreneur or business person reading this, seriously consider getting one.

There are reasons people like Oprah, Henry McKinnell (CEO of Pfizer), Meg Whitman (CEO of E-Bay), and David Pottrruck (CEO of Charles Schwab & Co.) use them. Tim Ferris of "The 4-Hour Workweek" and Noah Kagan, CEO of App Sumo and fellow author, have multiple coaches. I'm a coach4, and I still have one, and it's one of the reasons this book is being published in a timely fashion.

Now, you're ready for the final step. You have everything lined up now except for sharing it. This is where you get your cheerleaders and detractors.

SHARED: Only now, once it's all laid out, should you go ahead and share the goal and sign it. Remember, one of the things we learned from scientific research was that a man is more likely to achieve his goal if money or his reputation is on the line.

Don't forget. Sharing your goals is yet another form of accountability if you think about it.

So, get on Facebook™, your blog, forums, amongst your family, friends, and co-workers, and let everyone know what you

---

4 Never trust a coach who doesn't have a coach

intend to do and what you've pledged to lose if you don't stick to your guns.

There's also a place here to sign the documentation. A section of the book is coming up on honor, loyalty, and integrity. If you put your signature on that piece of paper, will you honor it, or are you just full of it?

It always amazed me that guys deserted from the Foreign Legion. When they went in and passed the physical, mental, and intelligence tests, they signed a piece of paper saying they would spend five years with the Legion. That signature was their word and their bond. To give up and go over the wall to get home is just beyond me. Once you sign, you stay. It's that simple.

In a recent workshop, an investment guru, Phil Town, gave a great example. He was talking about what happens if you're trying to convince people to invest with you and you have a terrible first month. He said you should tear that one up and hope for a better one next month, right? The crowd laughed, and several put their hands up to say yes, that's what they'd do. When they did, he said, "No, you just failed the character test. You should let everyone know you did badly because that's true. That truthfulness demonstrates your integrity."

I've provided a sample template you can complete in the following section. If you don't want to write in here, go to NickHughesCoaching.com and you can download PDFs there and fill them out at home.

You will notice the word promise in the forms—big word. Phil Town mentioned this one as well. He told us that a goal is okay, but while it makes the person feel better about themselves, it's not a serious commitment.

As he pointed out, if he said I have a goal to meet you tonight at 7 pm at the coffee shop, it's not really guaranteeing he'll be there, is it? He feels good about it, though, because he said it, which made us both happy. What would be a whole lot stronger would be a statement from him saying, "I promise I will meet you at the coffee shop at 7 pm."

So, are you promising to work toward these goals, or is it just pie-in-the-sky feel-good talk?

SAMPLE GOAL SHEET

I _____ have a goal to/of _____

_____

_____

_____

_____

_____

_____

and I PROMISE that I will accomplish it by _____

I absolutely want to achieve this goal because

_____

_____

_____

_____

_____

_____

_____

_____

The following are the steps I will take to achieve my goal.

1

_____

2

_____

3

_____

4

_____

5

_____

6

_____

7

_____

8

_____

9

_____

10

_____

The Resources I Already Have Are: _____

_____

_____

The Resources I Will Need to See It Through Are:

_____

_____

_____

_____

_____

For each of the planning steps, I will reward myself by/with

1

_____

2

_____

3

_____

4

_____

5

_____

6

_____

7

_____

8

_____

9

_____

10

_____

My accountability partner is _____

_____, and I have given

her/him two amounts of money made out to _____

_____ in the

amounts of _____ and

_____ respectively.

(S)He and I have signed a contract detailing that if I should fail to

achieve my goal by _____, then (s)he will cash

the (first) check(s). If I fail to achieve the ultimate goal by the

date _____ (s)he will forward the second check.

I have shared the goal with/on _____

_____

_____

_____

_____

_____

_____

Signed _____

Dated _____

Witnessed: _____

KEY POINTS

- Make a list of everything you want to have, be, see, and do in your lifetime.
- Break them down into short-term, medium-range, and long-term goals.
- Pick four to ten per year you want to work on.
- Use reverse engineering.
- Put them where you can see them on a regular basis.
- Review them often.
- Check you aren't focused too much on short-term or long-term goals.
- Pick your accountability partner well.
- Write the reason why this goal is important to you.

APPENDIX A

ACCOUNTABILITY PARTNER.

Make a list of potential accountability partners here. Remember, they will have to be somebody who will hold you accountable and follow through when you don't fulfill your commitments. It's no good if, because they're your buddy, or because you whine at them, or hit them with a guilt trip, they'll let you slide. I don't recommend using your significant other, family members, or friends. Use your business coach, attorney, or, as I mentioned earlier, me if you can't find anyone else.

It's pretty simple. Do you want this goal, or don't you? Are you serious, or are you a lightweight? As the bracelet from Grant Cardone says, "Don't be a little bitch."

Name: _____

Email: _____

Phone: _____

Will they? Yes: ☐   No: ☐

Did you give them the money & instructions?

Yes: ☐ No: ☐

Name: _____

Email: _____

Phone: _____

Will they? Yes: ☐   No: ☐

Did you give them the money & instructions?

Yes: ☐ No: ☐

Name: _____

Email: _____

Phone: _____

Will they? Yes: ☐   No: ☐

Did you give them the money & instructions?

Yes: ☐ No: ☐

See the website for a downloadable agreement between you and your accountability partner.

APPENDIX B

SHARED

I have shared my goals on the following social media and/or with the following people.

FB: ☐

X: ☐

Tik Tok: ☐

Instagram: ☐

Linked In: ☐

Other: ☐

Friends and family: ☐

I respond best to a support team or proving people wrong (circle one)

APPENDIX C

PLANNED

These are the steps to achieve my goal of….

In 3 years, I will: _____

In 2 years, I will: _____

In 1 year, I will: _____

In 9 months: _____

In 6 months: _____

In 3 months: _____

APPENDIX D

REWARDS

Intrinsic Rewards: _____

_____

_____

_____

_____

Extrinsic Rewards: _____

_____

_____

_____

_____

_____

_____

APPENDIX E

EMOTIONAL/EXCLUSIVE

I attest the goal of _____

_____

_____

_____

_____

_____ is mine and mine alone for me and by

me.

The reason (My Why) I need to accomplish this goal is because

_____

_____

_____

_____

_____

_____

REFERENCES

Grote, D., Knight, R., Clark, D., & Su, A. J. (2017, December 05). 3 Popular Goal-Setting Techniques Managers Should Avoid. Retrieved from https://hbr.org/2017/01/3-popular-goal-setting-techniques-managers-should-avoid.

How Starbucks Plans to Make an Impact by 2020 and Beyond. (April 24, 2017). Retrieved from https://news.starbucks.com/news/starbucks-2016-global-social-impact-report.

Kleingeld, A, Van Mierlo, H, & Arends, L. R. (2011). The Effect of Goal Setting on Group Performance: A Meta-Analysis . Journal of Applied Psychology, 96(6), 1289-304.

Locke, E. A. & Latham, G. P. (2006). New Directions in Goal-Setting Theory. Current Directions in Psychological Science, 15(5), 265-268.

Matthews, G. (2015). https://www.dominican.edu/academics/lae/undergraduate-programs/psych/faculty/assets-gail-matthews/researchsummary2.pdf.

AUTHOR'S GOALS

GOALS COMPLETED

Black belt in Judo

Black belt in Aikido

Black belt in Zen Do Kai

Black belt in Combat Karate

Box professionally

Unarmed Combat Instructor

Special Forces Soldier

Paratrooper

Commando

Frogman

Bodyguard to VIPs

Speak fluent French

See Russia

See Finland

See Switzerland

See Germany

Live in Africa

Get on national TV

Write a book

See England

See the Great Barrier Reef

Date Royalty

Own my own business

Meet Jim Rohn

Own a Porsche (twice).

Own a Rolex

Join Toastmasters

Win a speech competition

Get a pilot's license

Bodyguard Rock Stars

Ride a motorbike around the US

Sell paintings

Become a tattoo artist

Live in Europe

Get a tattoo

Speak professionally

Be featured by Paladin Press

Swim with Dolphins

Learn to cook

Drive 200mph

Have a book signing

Teach at Karate College

Meet Phil Town

Save someone's life

Turn someone's life around

Run a marathon

Parachute into the ocean

Visit the Great Barrier Reef

Visit Key West

To Start my Coaching Business

Certified in Hypnosis

Certified in NLP

GOALS STILL TO ACCOMPLISH

(but by the time you're reading these, I guarantee you at least five will have been achieved)

Own a house on the water

Speak fluent Spanish

Speak Mandarin

Speak fluent German

See Niagara Falls

See Mount Rushmore

Raft the Grand Canyon

Join NSA

Get a helicopter license

Meet Tony Robbins

Meet Dan Hardy

Meet Grant Cardone

Appear on Fire Nation Podcast

Speak at Lewis Howe's event

Own an H1 Alpha Hummer

Own a Rolex Challenge

Win the lottery

Appear in a major movie

Learn to play the piano

Have a recurring TV role

Publish my 1st novel

Publish We Are Legion

Publish my Bug in Bag book

Buy a plane

Own Rental Property

Appear on cover of Black Belt

Certified in Lefkoe Belief System

Appear on cover of Success Magazine

Have my novel optioned

Meet Arnold Schwarzenegger

Meet Seven Segal

Have a net worth of over $5M

Get invited to the White House

Own a condo at the beach

Play the guitar

Learn to Tango

ACKNOWLEDGMENTS

The very first person I wish to acknowledge is YOU. You have no idea what it means to an author, that you bought their book and took the time to read it. So thank you. It means a lot.

Now, nobody ever writes a book on their own. These are some of the people who helped me write this one. While I try to remember them all, there's probably someone I forgot to mention, and should that be the case, remember, I'm getting old. I've now reached the point where I can't remember where I parked my car, so don't be mad if I forgot you here.

Beta Readers: Alexander Capecci, David Brooks, Starr Kiser, John Hoover, Perry Slaton, Caroline Kone, Greg Oldham.

Cover Design: On the resource page at www.Nick-HughesCoaching dot com.

Special Mention: To Dr Andy Williams whose Udemy courses helped me build my website and write this. Best instructor on Udemy.

Formatter/Editor: Grace Michael

NOW THAT YOU'VE FINISHED

If you liked this book, please take a couple of minutes to log onto Amazon and leave a review. Your opinion matters and it helps others decide whether or not this humble effort is worth it.

It's especially critical for self-published authors like me because we don't have the backing of the big publishing houses who can throw money at promotions.

If you didn't like it please, let me know that too. It helps me know where I'm going wrong, and it makes the next book even better.

If you're on social media, feel free to let your mates know about it. If it helps them achieve their goals they're never going to forget you pointed them in the right direction.

If you want to reach me personally feel free. I love hearing from my readers, and, unlike some big name authors, I'll always take time to reply. You can do that on the www.Nick-HughesCoaching page.

Thanks a million. Peace

INDEX

147

www.ingramcontent.com/pod-product-compliance
Lightning Source LLC
Chambersburg PA
CBHW030936090426
42737CB00007B/449